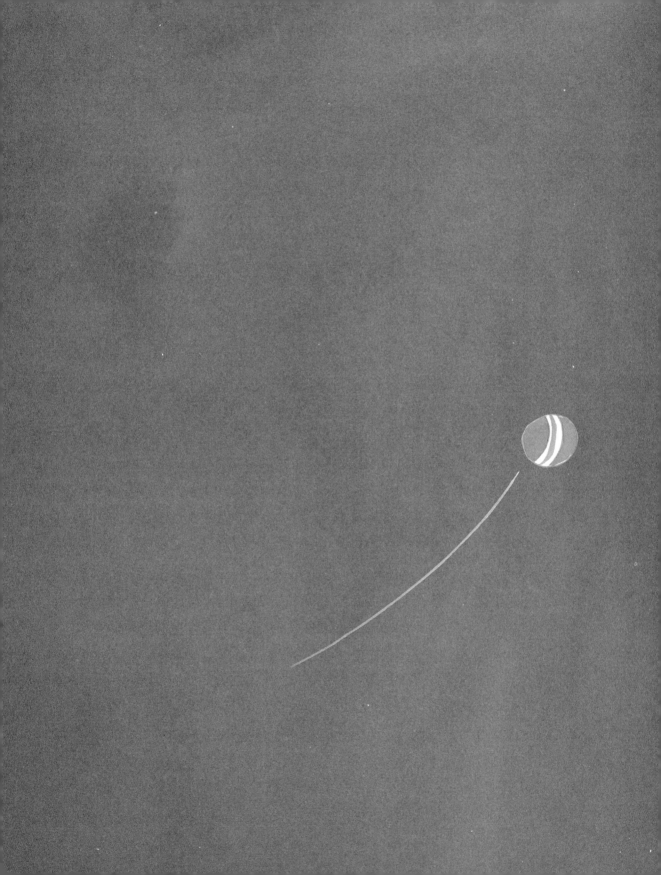

Well Played

Well Played

THE ULTIMATE GUIDE TO AWAKENING YOUR FAMILY'S PLAYFUL SPIRIT

Meredith Sinclair

WM

WILLIAM MORROW

An Imprint of HarperCollinsPublishers

HarperCollins books may be purchased for educational, business, or sales promotional use. For information please e-mail the Special Markets Department at SPsales@harpercollins.com.

All illustrations copyright Anne Keenan Higgins.

FIRST EDITION

Designed by Leah Carlson-Stanisic

Watercolor background panel by ninanaina/Shutterstock, Inc.

Library of Congress Cataloging-in-Publication Data has been applied for.

ISBN 978-0-06-239136-0

16 17 18 19 20 OV/RRD 10 9 8 7 6 5 4 3 2 1

For **Ann**, the most playful friend I ever had. "Cheers!"
For **Jon**, **Maxwell**, and **Truman**. Our 4-pack is my
favorite thing in the whole wide world, and the inspiration
for it all.

Contents

Introduction

Playfulness and I go waaaaaay back.

[Insert dreamy, 1970s flashback effect here]

"Merrily." That was my nickname as a young girl. Merrily we roll along, Merrily, merrily, merrily, merrily, life is but a dream . . . you get the picture.

Merrily is a mash-up of Meredith and Lee, the first and middle monikers on my birth certificate. I don't recall many folks calling me Meredith when I was little, except my prim and proper grandmother on my dad's side, and my parents when I was in deep shih tzu.

The *Oxford English Dictionary* defines "merrily" as an adverb, meaning "in a cheerful manner, without giving consideration to possible problems or future implications" (a sentiment that also happens to be a part of the definition of play . . . the state of being happily lost in an experience, with no cares about what comes next).

Clueless as I was to the word's meaning, I fully embodied this lively nickname. When people from my childhood describe how they remember me, the words "happy" and "playful" often show up. I was the fun and sunshiny one, even when my world was in turmoil. I was the little girl who made friends easily, who loved to romp in the mud, sing myself to sleep, and frolic in the woods, the creek, or around any sports field on which my two older brothers got to play. Pre–Title IX meant holding my own with the boys on soccer and Little League teams. And I was totally down with that. We were called tomboys back then. Thankfully, athletic, adventurous girls who enjoy playing in the dirt, climbing trees, and throwing an occasional fastball are now just called girls.

Growing up in a small western Pennsylvania town in the 1970s and '80s, where everyone knew everyone and everything was a bike ride away, we had tremendous freedom to roam and play with our pals until the streetlights flickered, our banana-seat bikes blew a tire, or we heard our mom's distant yet powerful voice cutting through dusk like a siren, letting us know it was time to hustle home. We didn't have followers and we weren't fueled by "likes," and our social networks consisted of the five friends whose phone numbers we had memorized. And yet we managed to create deeply connected and influential friendships, and there was always someone with whom to play.

After high school graduation, I ran headfirst into becoming an elementary school teacher. And I was in a hurry, graduating from college in three years with honors. I had found my happy place, a challenging yet cheerful and playful profession, and I simply couldn't wait to marry my high school sweetheart and get life started. I taught for several years, got a master's degree, led classes at the Children's Museum of Pittsburgh, and worked as an educational consultant at a PBS station in Pittsburgh (right above *Mister Rogers' Neighborhood*!). We eventually moved to Chicago for my husband Jon's dream producing job with the *Oprah Winfrey Show*. We were adventurous and young and very playful indeed.

As I set up life in Chicago, started having children, and held down the fort while Jon made his long and very time-intensive climb up the TV producer ladder, there came a slow-growing but definite shift in my adventurous and playful spirit. It didn't happen right away or all at once, but it happened nonetheless.

With the birth of our first son, I started to become anxious and worrisome. I suddenly needed to control everything. It was a gradual shift from my former happy-go-lucky self and only accelerated with the birth of our second son four years later. I adored raising our two young boys. I wanted to be home with them, and I knew I was blessed to have that choice, but with my husband's demanding work schedule, I was going it alone most of the time. I was downright exhausted and made no time for anything resembling play.

I began to focus on managing the chaos of life instead of enjoying any part of it. I was that "Quiet down," "Did you wash your hands long enough?," "This house is a pigsty!," "BE CAREFUL!" kind of mom. Constantly. I suddenly loathed messes and disorder, and loud and unruly play.

Where had Merrily run off to?

Around this time, I began doing this new thing called "blogging" as a way of expressing what I was working through in my stay-at-home mom days. I also attended my first blogging conference called BlissDom. It was there that I had my epiphany.

A man named Kevin Carroll, author of *Rules of the Red Rubber Ball*, was the keynote speaker. Through story after delightful story, Mr. Carroll explained how creativity, passion, and, most important, playfulness had changed his life for the better. I wept in my seat as I listened, and knew I had discovered the cause of my unhappiness. I had completely forgotten how to be playful. I realized I was actually jealous of my kids, and that's why their in-my-face, unabashed, joyous playfulness was actually pissing me off. Children are often a shiny reflection of what we're doing well and not so well in our lives, aren't they?

It was time for me to make a shift.

When I got home from the conference, I began devouring every book I could find on play research, and focused my writing and website on the pursuit of a more play-FULL life. I visited the National Museum of Play, did many talks on the importance of playfulness in our parenting lives at conferences and for parenting groups, started writing a playful column for *Chicago Parent* magazine, and began doing TV segments on playful living both locally and nationally on the *Today* show. It's been a yellow brick road of realization.

Here are a few things I've learned along the way:

* We are born knowing how to play.
* Playfulness is innate, God-given, and everlasting.
* Being well played, while seeming a bit frivolous, is in fact quite vital to a happy and healthy physical, emotional, and mental state.
* Play is the primary way we discover and make sense of the world as children.
* The game-changing goodness we experience from play as children is available to us and just as beneficial throughout our entire lives.
* We can run, but we can't hide. Our primal desire for play never flags. It's the best seeker ever, and it will always find you.

4

"Play is the work of children," as Mr. Rogers said. But even though we may not need play to learn as much as we once did, we never, ever outgrow the need or desire to get swept up in a playful experience. And we are always better for it.

Philosophers from Plato to Jean Piaget to Friedrich Schiller have all acknowledged that play is the catalyst for all art, invention, new connections, and innovation. Play ignites our minds in ways only it can. It's a whole cerebral cortex/prefrontal lobe of the brain kind of thing. Not to get all scientific on you, but that portion of our noggin gets all bossy when it comes to things like complex cognitive behavior, personality expression, decision making, planning, judgment, and moderating social behavior. It basically orchestrates our thoughts and actions. (No biggie.)

And when our prefrontal cortex is all "Let's play!," it's like fireworks on the Fourth of July . . . *Ka-boom!* Mind blown. Playful folks tend to be more cognitively flexible, adaptable, and sharp. *Bam!*

In his book *Play: How It Shapes the Brain, Opens the Imagination, and*

Invigorates the Soul, Dr. Stuart Brown (one of my favorite play gurus) explains that the opposite of play is not in fact work, as you might suspect, but rather depression. DEPRESSION, people!

In his research, Dr. Brown has found that when denied play for long periods of time, our emotional well-being is "compromised." (I'm totally not cool with a compromised well-being, how about you?)

He's discovered that if we go without play for too long we become "anhedonic," or incapable of experiencing sustained pleasure. I mean . . . who the HECK wants that? In Dr. Brown's words, "To miss out on play is to miss the harvest of a well-lived life." Amen and amen.

With modern families busier and more high-strung than ever, it's quite easy to succumb to the notion that there is simply no time or necessity to "play around." But guess what? There are some nasty effects of a little something called play deprivation. And they ain't pretty. Seriously, Google it. We're talking all sorts of bad.

Purposeful, intentional, and childlike playfulness either with others or on our own unlocks our ability to get drenched in what makes our hearts and minds sing, and who we truly are under all of our hard work's achievements, titles, and responsibilities.

Bottom line: Being playful is a key component in making us happier, healthier, more present and connected in all of our relationships. With our kids, our partners, our family members, our friends, our workmates, and our own often overlooked play-deprived *selves*. 1,000% Truth.

One of my favorite quotes is, "You can discover more about a person in one hour of play than you can in a year of conversation." Preach.

Playing together requires trust and acceptance, letting down our guard. There is very little, if any, ego allowed in playfulness.

And let's be honest: we often perceive people more truly and clearly during a game of bocce than over a bottle of Beaujolais. We need to shut down the devices, check our egos at the door, and allow our inner eight-year-olds to come barreling through.

Just as we are urged to be well fed, well hydrated, well educated, well connected, well trained . . . we must also give ourselves permission to be well played. It's a matter of health, happiness, and good clean *fun*.

I hope you use this book as your permission slip.

Here, I'll even sign it for you:

_____ has my permission to stop working so
[Your name here]   hard and start playing a little harder.

Seriously,

Meredith Sinclair

"Merrily"

"Home is for
free expression
not good
impressions"

- YOURS, MINE AND OURS

Your Playground

Are you the "obsessively neat and tidy" type?

Are you that parent who hovers over your young scribes, cleaning up their playful "mess-terpieces" as they are literally mid–glue sticking, LEGO building, or dress-upping? Does the thought of finger paint make your throat begin to close? Does every one of your board games still have all of its pieces and its own alphabetically arranged spot on the designated board game shelf? Do you pride yourself on how perfectly perfect it all looks? All the time? Just in case someone drops by?

And then you go to bed deeply wishing you were enjoying your home more? Yeah, I've been that parent.

Or are you the "free to be you and me" type?

Are you that parent encouraging your precious bohemian wildflowers to totally TA-RASH the house on a daily basis in the name of creativity and free play? Does the thought of color-coding or labeling anything, ever, make your skin break out in completely unstructured hives? Does your house always look like Hurricane Toddler just swept through? All the time? And you secretly pray that no one ever just drops by?

And then you go to bed deeply wishing you were enjoying your home more? Yeah, I've been that parent too.

Picture-Perfect vs. Freakin' Pigsty— There's a Better Way

After eighteen years of sharing my playground with children, and spending years as an early childhood educator before that, there is one thing I know for sure when it comes to creating, and then sharing, our beloved space with small humans: There is a very happy medium between picture-perfect and a freakin' pigsty. I call it "playfully designed." It's a domestic sweet spot right smack dab in the middle, where playfulness and esthetics hold hands and sing "Kumbaya" around a really ridiculous, yet meaningful, drum circle.

Classroom studies have shown that children don't really thrive in environments of utter chaos, clutter confusion, and tornadic storms of stuff. I believe this goes for grown-ups too, for aren't we all those same children underneath? Even during messy activities like finger painting, shaving cream sculptures, and dress-up props upon dress-up props in my preschool classroom, the children enjoyed it much more when there was a picket fence of structure and predictability surrounding it all.

Alternatively, most of us don't fully relax and open ourselves up to playful experiences—with or without our kids—when we're constantly having panic attacks about every disruption in our mess-free force, or dreading how many times we're going to have to sing that mind-numbing "Clean Up Song" at the end of it all. You know the one, "Clean up, clean up, everybody, everywhere" . . . sticks fork in eye. Glitter is both heaven and hell coming out of that little shaker bottle, isn't it?

But take a deep breath with me now . . . inhaaaaaale . . . exhaaaaaaale . . .

I'd like to let you in on a little "playfully designed" secret I learned during my days as a teacher in the early childhood classroom.

When I had my first son, Maxwell, I was just coming off my job as a second-grade teacher at a progressive, play-based, laboratory school on the North Shore of Chicago. Lab schools are private schools that are connected to universities or colleges. I went to a university that had a lab school attached to it, which was invaluable in my own teacher preparation because I got amazing hands-on experience just by being next door.

Unlike my previous teaching posts, which were at very traditional public schools where "order in the court" was often valued over creativity in the classroom, Baker Demonstration School had it figured out, and changed me for the better as an educator of young children.

It was there, as a second- and third-grade classroom teacher and then as a teacher in their early childhood program, that I discovered the delicious cocktail of playfulness plus education: the natural desire to play, mixed with a healthy shot of academia and a splash of "order."

Parents would enter my classroom and see a "mess" of cardboard boxes, construction paper, and other creative debris littering the desks and floor as we worked to construct buildings for our makeshift town, or children using costumes and sets and scripts to act out a significant moment in history, all loud and collaborative and unruly in the best of ways. What they were seeing was an environment that was very carefully, thoughtfully, and playfully designed. It was all on purpose. It was neither picture-perfect nor a freakin' pigsty. Because none of us really function well in either of those extreme environments, now do we?

As teachers at Baker, we were encouraged to tap into the children's natural inclination toward play and discovery, while infusing all of the standard curriculum requirements we had to meet. It was in fact messy and seemingly unorganized at times, but never out of control. Our students flourished in this kind of learning playground. And so did we.

We played hard and welcomed big bouts of educational mess-making, and then, out of respect for our beloved space, we equally enjoyed putting things back in order to be ready for our next adventure.

The strategy I used to create a playfully designed environment in my early childhood classroom managing three-, four-, and five-year-olds is the same strategy I've used over the last eighteen years with my home-room of two: my boys, Maxwell and Truman.

When I decided to "stay home" and be the primary caregiver for my kids, I wanted my home to be a playfully designed place of mind-opening, creativity-fostering, inviting spaces, with pops of messy magic sprinkled heavily on top.

If you're someone who needs a perfectly polished household to feel happy and safe, inviting more playfulness into your home may require a loosening up of the "what will people think" pressure you might be under. Sorry, but you're probably driving your family crackers too, BTW.

You are.

I've gone through periods of severe home-keeping anal retention myself over the years, and it's just no fun. For you, or anyone with whom you live.

Just remind yourself: NO ONE LIVES IN THE POTTERY BARN CATALOG! THEY'RE SO TOTALLY FAKE, Y'ALL.

You've undoubtedly heard it before, but let me say it again.

All the tidying and to-do lists you feel compelled to complete will still be annoyingly waiting for you with bated breath when you've finished playing. Seriously, those pesky to-dos NE-VER go away. And honestly, they could really benefit from a little vacay now and again. We give them far too much power, and they are becoming a bit entitled.

In the words of every mom I ever met when my kids were little: "You will one day look back and wish you'd chilled the heck out and played more, rather than managed, and tidied, and perfected more." And they were so totally right.

Clearly, embracing the concept of a playfully designed home can be a bit harder of a pill to swallow for the severely tidy.

But if your design style can be described best as "eclectic, midcentury,

kid crap everywhere," it's time to make a slight adjustment as well. Remember, the goal here is somewhere in the middle of these two extremes. A place of spirit-soothing order, style, and beauty, which also invites those who live there, and those who visit, to come out and play as often as possible.

Are you ready to create a really well-played home base?

Then grab your playground balls and let's go!

Inspecting Your Grounds

Creating the home of your dreams always begins with a thorough inspection. Before you close on a house or do any of the moving in and decorating, you must first take a really good look around to see what you're workin' with. It's vital to take stock of what needs to be repaired, what needs replacing, and what simply isn't working for you any longer and needs pitching. We're going to take the same approach as we strive to create a more energizing and stimulatingly playful space for you and the other humans with whom you dwell.

Use the home inspection checklist (opposite) to help you take stock of how your home is already playfully jammin', and what bits and baubles need a little TLC. Pencils ready?

Place a check mark on the statements that describe the state of your dwelling space.

- ☐ Making it through my kids' playroom is like an episode of *American Ninja Warrior.*

- ☐ No one is permitted to truly LIVE in my living room.

- ☐ Finger paint, Play-Doh, and glitter are the devil's spawn, and not welcome here.

- ☐ The largest design motifs in my bedroom are unfolded laundry and LEGO minefield.

- ☐ If a stranger walked into my kitchen the first question might be "Who's the president of this fraternity house?"

- ☐ Toys "R" so not Us . . . out of sight, out of mind.

- ☐ A place for everything and everything in its place . . . or someone loses an appendage.

- ☐ The neighbors on my street couldn't pick me out of a lineup.

- ☐ My dining room table might be mistaken for a Geek Squad gathering.

- ☐ My feng shui leaves little or no space for play.

Purposeful Pops of Playfulness

"If you build it they will come"

I had a strong desire when my boys were very small to create a home that encouraged spontaneous frivolity, yet would still be a place that was enjoyable and not a constant mess-ola. That desire required me to let go and shift my expectations for my family's space. When my kids were babies and toddlers and preschoolers, our biggest battle was controlling the sheer amount of playthings and equipment amassed during a typical childhood. An even bigger challenge at that age is to allow ourselves to join our kids in their most happy place a little more often. To manage less and engage more. And another challenge is in keeping your space from looking like a Target toy aisle just keeps hurling all over your design scheme.

One of the things my husband came up with early on in our parenthood was to be semi-discerning about the number of toys and other playthings we brought into our home, and the types of playthings we suggested family members purchase as gifts when they asked. One strategy that helped us tremendously was choosing three or four main brands or types of toys to collect, and then building our collection within those brands. For example, the main "sets" we chose when our boys were little were LEGO, PLAYMOBIL, and Thomas the Tank Engine trains. When anyone asked what they could buy our boys for holiday or birthday gifts, we picked a set or accessory from one of those brands. This worked brilliantly to keep the toys from taking over our home, and because we knew the boys already loved these sets, it was a win-win for all. Of course we also received special items to supplement those sets, like a multipurpose art easel, big gym mats for the basement, bikes, ride-ons, Play-Doh, Crayola crayons, craft supplies, instruments, etc. But keeping our brands in mind made it significantly easier to create an organized and simplified play and living space.

As my boys traveled through the elementary, middle, and now high school years, the challenge became more about keeping their playful spirits ignited in the midst of schoolwork, homework, and adult-led extracurricular activities, like organized sports and clubs. I realized that if I wanted to keep our home a playful place, I needed to purposefully lay a playful foundation and then provide creative experiences that were naturally inviting. The minute you try and push anything on your kids, it becomes extremely unappealing. Toddlers and teenagers are our best examples of this. They could teach a freakin' master class on the art of resistance.

My hope is that, by using some of these simple ideas, you'll discover something that will help you and your family digitally disconnect to playfully reconnect during the time you spend together. These suggestions aren't meant to add to the unattainable parental mountaintop that is bento box school lunches that look like scenes from *Frozen* or those

spectacularly designed playrooms that no one has ever been allowed to actually play in, ever. I'm looking at you again, Pottery Barn.

What we are after are intentional nuggets of playful design in our homes, which send the message to everyone who enters that this is a safe place to let your fun self free and your guard way down.

Now it's time to add those "purposeful pops of playfulness" throughout your home!

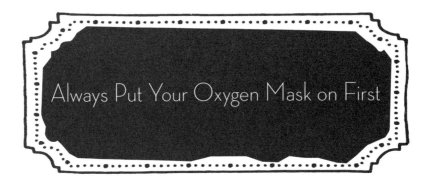

Always Put Your Oxygen Mask on First

Our homes are the ultimate expression of who we are and what we hold dear. Or at least they should be.

Whether you live in an apartment in the city, a farmhouse on a country lane, or Barbie's Dreamhouse in the burbs, your home should "rise up to greet you when you walk through the door." I first heard someone say that on an *Oprah* show years ago when I had young children ruling my roost, and it was an "aha moment" for me as I realized that we should be intentional about that place we call home.

Our homes should RISE UP to greet us. RISE UP!

Imagine . . .

Is your home rising up to greet you when you walk through the door, or barely glancing up from its device to mumble "Oh, you again"? Over the past several years I have been trying to find simple and inexpensive ways to help my house rise up, to playfully greet me throughout the day. I spend a whole lot of time in my home as a writer and blogger, and I was tired of simply looking at my surroundings all the time in terms of what needed cleaning up, organizing, or fixing.

Again, creating a beautifully playful space isn't about spending a bunch of money, hiring fancy decorators, or making your place Pinterest worthy. Nope, it's about adding delicious dollops of joy that light you up, make your soul sing, and set fire to your playful spirit, even while you're washing the dishes.

5 Playful Design Nuggets That Are All About ME

Here are five things that I have incorporated into my home that help me tap into my playful spirit when I need it most. They're simple, but highly effective. I encourage you to identify and lasso up the play-pushin' things that will help you connect with your own play-full-est self within your own everydayness.

1 **EVERYTHING BUT THE KITCHEN SINK.** I keep a pretty tray near my kitchen sink stocked with yummy-smelling dish soaps and hand soaps (Williams-Sonoma's Spiced Chestnut is my FAVORITE for autumn), whimsical scrubbers and brushes, and a deliciously scented candle. I frequently pop on happy music when I have to spend time at the sink, and as I'm scouring away at that gross gunk caked onto my pots and pans, I take a

little time to play in the suds! I also have a window ledge right in front of my sink where I place playful quotes, happy pictures, and other reminders of things that bring me joy—stones from Lake Michigan, air plants, trinkets my boys have made me, etc.

2 NO WIRE HANGERS! Okay, so maybe I have a couple of wire hangers in my closet, and it's never perfectly tidy or magazine worthy. But my closet *is* playful and fashionably fun. After reading a very popular book on tidying one's home, I decided that nothing in my closet would be permitted to stay unless it

"sparked joy." So I slashed and burned, thanked stuff for its service, and Goodwilled. Then I turned the back of my closet door into a massive style "look book" collage. Remember ripping out looks from magazines you loved when you were a teenager, and then plastering them on your wall? Yeah, that. Now my inner teenager comes busting through every time I open the door. Call me, and I'll come over and help you tear up *Vogue* and *InStyle*.

3. **A BRIGHT YELLOW DESK AND A BUBBLE MA-CHINE.** Both of these things can be found in my home office, and both bring me significant joy. Adding a few brightly colored furnishings or accessories, especially where least expected, instantly evokes playfulness and creativity in your home. And it's impossible to not be amused by bub-bles in the air. It's especially good if you can get away with having these in your workspace. All work and no playfulness makes Meredith a total bee-atch.

4. **MOOD SWINGS.** One of my very favorite things is the swing that hangs in my boys' bedroom at our Michigan cottage. Their room was built over the garage and has a super-high ceiling with big beams overhead. When we were designing and decorating their space—a room we call the barracks—I knew I had finally found the perfect place for an indoor swing. If you follow me on Instagram, you know I'm a bit of a swingaholic (a tall tree, two lengths of rope, and a butt-length piece of wood—bliss). I found a small but sturdy wooden swing from IKEA and hung it beside the two bunk beds in their room. Some of my best nights are the ones I've spent reading the Hardy Boys aloud, or

just talking to them about their days and lives, as I swing and swing and swing beside them.

5. **RUB-A-DUB-DUB, STAY OUT OF MY TUB.** Every night, and sometimes each morning, I take a bath, preferably with mounds of bubbles. It's a thing. I inherited my love for the tub from my mom, who as far back as I can remember took nightly soaks too. I make my tub as inviting as possible, because I like to play in the tub as much as a two-year-old does. To set the scene, I adorn my bath with fun salts that look like ice cream sundaes and root beer floats from a shop called Smitten, I keep pretty grown-up coloring books and watercolor pencils nearby, I still overuse Mr. Bubble bubble bath like I did when I was five, and there may be rubber duckies involved.

Play Maker 5 WAYS TO KEEP YOUR HOME STYLISH, BEAUTIFUL, AND INVITINGLY PLAYFUL

Nate Berkus, bestselling author and interior designer

1. Embrace whimsy in design, but be careful not to venture into theme-room territory. A handmade woolen stuffed animal or carved animal figural in a serious room always makes me smile.

2. Try not to take the design process too seriously; sometimes an impulse buy or an odd, original lamp can make the space seem more sophisticated and less boring.

3. Use color where it won't cause you to pawn your car title if you change your mind—a red lampshade or a wild-patterned pillow costs a lot less than a sofa in the "donate" pile.

4. Break some rules, experiment with your floor plan. The best and most original interiors throughout history are the ones where someone took a risk.

5. Kill it on Etsy/eBay/your local flea: Nothing changes the feeling of a space more than a GREAT, one-of-a-kind accessory.

Jenga as Modern Art

About a year ago we got a new media cabinet for under our TV. As I was cleaning out the old one, I realized we hadn't touched half the really cool games and building toys I had stored there. I have always tried to pick and keep toys that could grow with my kids, and looking at all the closed-up boxes of beautiful manipulative design and building toys in that cupboard,

I wondered if they could have a second life with my growing boys, who just didn't run to the LEGO bin like they used to. I knew it would never happen if I simply moved these items to the new cabinet and shut the door again. I decided instead to place a big beautiful wire bowl on the coffee table and fill it with one kind of plaything. I started with Jenga blocks. Released from their torn and tattered box and presented in a new way, they instantly became a modern design accessory that cried out to be messed with. My boys, their friends, and mine would saunter in and react as though they were seeing an old friend after a long hiatus.

I now replace that bowl's contents every month or so with a new manipulative. This simple shift in playful presentation not only repurposes creative playthings my kids have forgotten about, it encourages us to gather in the living room, look up from our alluring devices, and do a little more gabbing and building, rather than swiping and sending.

Play-Inducing Things to Dump into a Decorative Bowl on Your Coffee Table

* LEGO bricks
* K'NEX building pieces
* Lincoln Logs
* Dominos
* ZOOB blocks
* Colorforms
* Magformers
* Small wooden blocks
* Wooden marble machine pieces and one marble
* Vintage wooden Tinkertoys
* Jenga blocks

* Toy soldiers
* Stringing beads and pretty twine

No one can resist a big bowl of playfulness plopped down in plain view. Repurposing your older kids' most interesting toys of old and turning them into a modern-art installation invites everyone who sits down in your living room to reconnect with their inner child.

Pump Up the Jams

"Medicine heals the body, music heals the soul."

—ANONYMOUS

The music you choose to play or not to play in your home has a significant effect on your sweet abode and everybody in it. Music of all makes and models has been a big part of our home forever. In fact, our house feels slightly awkward when the music isn't on, like Ernie without Bert.

Want to instantly shift the vibe of your place? Put the needle on the record. The right musical outburst can take a bad day and knock it right on its B side.

People talk about having dance parties in their kitchens, but how many of us ACTUALLY bust a move while making breakfast, do the Dougie during dinner prep, and the Nae Nae before bedtime? Really? Have you ever spontaneously cranked up the Spotify

and encouraged everyone to stop what they're doing and kick it for just ten minutes?

Every single time we blast a vibe-lifting, fun tune on our sound system and act like dancing fools, the antidepressant decibels in our home bust through the roof.

Happy, encouraging music during the morning rush or throughout the after-school nuttiness helps to level out the stress and remind us that most of the yucky, messy stuff of life really isn't cause for alarm. I have playlists on my phone titled "Lighten Up, Man," "This Day Sucks Lollipops," and "Mama's Gonna Blow" for when everyone needs a little lightening up. As your kids get a little older and a lot more self-conscious, these idiotic dance parties will both embarrass them fully and remind them that here at home, they can act a fool and ain't nobody gonna put it on Facebook, and that your home is a safe place to let the world fall away and play.

Every Snapshot Has a Story

I've come up with a way to use all of those vintage family photos for more than just #TBTs on Instagram.

My kids were little dudes in the days before smartphone addiction, Facebook, and Instagram. It was a very different world back then, my friend. I may not have photos of EVERY SINGLE moment of their young lives, but the photos I do have are precious and able to be held in my hands. At the risk of sounding like a ninety-year-old, I am actually glad I didn't have the availability of viewing my kids' young lives through a

smartphone lens. I totally would have over-Instagrammed them too. I often wonder how this young generation perceives their parents constantly putting a phone up to them all day long. I guess we'll find out in twenty years when they all start writing books . . .

But back to the point, I have always been obsessed with family photos. Ask my mother-in-law, whose photo books of my now husband's childhood I used to pull out and pore over for hours every time I visited them. Those photo books gave me a beautiful picture of the life my husband had before me, and what my future kids might look like in second grade.

We now live in a world of nonstop digital images, stored on cameras and scrolled through quickly, that always feel slightly once removed, since "clicking through" is quite different from holding and savoring. Tactile images of your family, both immediate and extended, can be a magical tool for all sorts of playful activities. Instead of simply storing your shots in the ether, gather the paper pictures you may have, or print out a hearty batch that are floating around in the Cloud, and use them as an invitation to reconnect and reminisce.

One of my favorite things to do with our "old" photos is to throw a bunch in a big bowl on our dining room table or in a basket on the kitchen island and let everyone get lost in some real, live "snap chats." We pull photos from the basket and tell stories about what was happening in them.

Playing together doesn't always mean physically romping around together. Verbal playfulness can be just as fun and engaging. One of my new absolute favorite ways to turn digital photos into something tactile is through a company called Chatbooks. They take your Instagram feed and, for under ten bucks, turn your photos into small, beautiful paperback books that look stunning on your shelf and are easy to pull down and devour.

Musical Dares and Family Jam Sessions

Start a collection of musical instruments for your home . . . even if nobody takes lessons or has a lick of musical talent.

While I'll grab any microphone and take over a karaoke stage or open-mic night, I am not what one might call musically inclined. To my credit, I did spend many weeks attempting to learn to play the guitar when I was a preschool teacher, because I wanted to be able to have sing-alongs with my students. I painfully learned a few chords . . . just enough to get us through "Froggy Went a-Courtin'" and "This Land Is Your Land," slowly, but surely.

To my three- and four-year-old students, though, I was Hendrix. They didn't give a hoot how mediocre I was as long as I kept singing and playing and handing out the preschool crack that is rhythm sticks and tambourines.

Since my kids were very young, I have been slowly collecting a variety of easy-to-play instruments to simply have around.

And over the years, going from filling baskets with plastic drums, shakers, and recorders to real instruments of all shapes and sizes, family "jam seshes" have become one of my son Truman's most frequent requests. He begs for everyone to participate, usually when it's slightly inconvenient or we all have more important things to do. But when we take twenty minutes in the midst of the after-dinner chaos to each grab a music maker, sit around the living room, and make up a tune, it's pure ridiculous fun. And then, we're on our way back to busy town.

The key is having a batch of instruments readily available and then forcing yourself to say yes when asked to play along, or starting the jam session yourself . . . even when you don't particularly feel like it.

Especially when you don't particularly feel like it. Start playing an instrument out of nowhere and watch the moths gather to your off-pitch flame. Your kids will find you freakish and irresistible all at once.

Plus, a collection of beautiful instruments serves as a "well, aren't *we* just artistic" art display in your living room. They'll make you feel like the Partridge Family. So there's that.

eBay is your friend when it comes to scoring interesting and inexpensive instruments. Here are a few of our favorites:

10 Easy Instruments to Have in Your "We're Not a Musical Family" Repertoire

* A ukelele
* A harmonica
* A tambourine or two
* A bongo drum
* A drum box. This is our latest acquisition, and I'm actually really good at this instrument. (It's a box you beat on with your hands and it makes different tones. Not rocket science.)
* A used acoustic guitar
* An electric keyboard
* Shakers. Put two cups of rice in a Pringles can, and poof! An instant rhythm section.
* Rhythm sticks
* An Autoharp. Possibly the most fun instrument for amateurs.

Make Room for Roughhousing

One of the best kid gifts we ever received from a grandparent was a set of big foldable gym mats for our basement. We have two boys and a big, carpeted basement that is perfect for wrestling, tumbling, flipping, bouncing, and roughhousing.

Now, I have to admit to you all that I am by nature a "Be careful!" kind of mom. I used to say it so much that my husband finally told me that I might as well be saying "Jiminy Cricket" because the boys heard "Be careful!" so much, it meant absolutely nothing. So I started saying "Be safe!" instead (baby steps). Because if you holler safety commands at your children four hundred times per minute, they will never ever get hurt. Right?

To save my voice, make room for a little personal peace of mind, and allow my boys to be boys, we got some big tumbling mats

to cover the basement floor. And then we bought moon bouncers, carpet slides, boxing gloves, yoga balls, a punching bag, etc. Stacking couch pillows up and jumping and tumbling over them works well too. #UseWhatYouHAVE

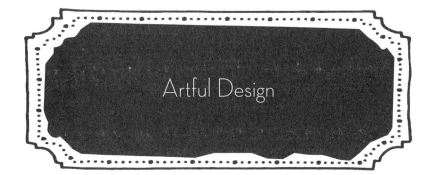

Artful Design

A Gallery of Artwork Encourages More Artwork ... from Everyone

I designed my first-floor powder room as something of an art gallery for the moderately talented folks with whom I dwell. I had a skilled painter color every wall with a rich lacquered gold, and I found vintage gold frames at tag sales and antique shops to house both our homemade art and pieces we've purchased. Every time I step into that powder room it makes me want to paint or draw or create. I love the idea of framing our family's art and creative expression as beautifully as possible.

Turn your home's art gallery into a family project. Kids, like adults, are way more into anything when they help create it.

Find an ideal spot for your playful expressions to be displayed, and then work together to make it *très* beautiful. If you need inspiration, go scan Pinterest for five minutes. Then click away, and make it your own.

PUSHPIN WALL ART

What You'll Need

* A picture frame, size is your choice
* Black foam board
* 300 to 500 brass or gold thumbtacks

Directions

1. Cut your foam board to fit inside your picture frame.

2. Trace your design onto your foam board with a pencil.

3. Start pinning!

4. Place the foam into the frame as you would a picture and hang it on the wall.

Tips:

* Keep your message simple. The larger you're able to make the letters, the easier they'll be to create with pins. Try "Home Sweet Home," "Play," or your family's last name.
* For a more contemporary look, paint a stretched canvas and use that as your pinning board.

Everybody Paints

Nab your family an inexpensive tabletop easel and keep it set up in a corner of the kitchen, on a sunporch, on the back deck, in the family room, wherever you have an uncarpeted spot slightly out of the way. Even if you have tweens and teens who think they are SO too old for that fo'shizzle, even if you have not one artistic bone in your body, set it up anyway. Stock it with various paints, brushes, art books, and still-life inspiration (I'm looking at *you*, bowl of fruit). If your kids aren't interested, create a tabletop studio just for you, and act sort of protective of your setup. Playing hard to get works great for reluctant, tech-obsessed tweens. They usually want what they think you don't want them to have. When they finally cave and pick up a paintbrush, hang their masterpieces all over the walls in the kitchen for a week. And yours too. Why do we stop hanging up our own artwork just because we grow up?

The Tablecloth of Awesome

Ditch that grown-up tablecloth or fancy runner you've got covering your dining room table and roll out a swath of butcher paper or chalkboard paper down the center of your table instead. I found both of these at a store called Paper Source, but craft stores have them too.

Once you've covered the table, add a pretty vessel filled with colorful markers, vibrant pencils, chalk, or chalkboard pens. Then have your family write, draw, decorate, and doodle all over the inviting new table-runner. There are lots of playful ways to use this creative table covering, and with every artful addition it will get more delightful and delicious. Here are some ideas for how to use your tablecloth of awesome:

1. Write five playful and thought-provoking questions for each family member to answer by dinnertime.
2. Ask everyone to make up a four-line silly poem or haiku and add it to the mix.
3. Fill it with compliments for other family members.
4. Write five things that were totally AWESOME about your day.
5. Throw down some washable-ink pads and a slew of rubber stamps and let 'em ink it up.
6. Jot down a bunch of witty riddles for your family to try and figure out over breakfast.
7. Create a collective, intermingling doodle that everyone adds to throughout the week.
8. Write the beginning line of a story and have your family add one line at a time to keep the story rolling.

9. Use your paper tablecloth for your next fancy dinner party or holiday function, encouraging your guests to color during dinner. Game changer.
10. Buy a batch of inexpensive Crayola watercolor sets, place one at each table setting, and plan some evenings of dessert and Degas.

Make Room for a "Creativity Cupboard"

Inviting more open-ended, playful creativity into the personal playground you call home means having a whole bunch of seemingly random "stuff" with which to create. As a teacher of young children and then as a mom of my own, I can tell you firsthand and without doubt that the most playfully creative endeavors of children are the ones they dream up themselves. We are but facilitators. And often that involves simply having materials to make their imaginative creations come to life. With kids turning more and more to the instant gratification of digital devices, now more than ever we need to provide opportunities to make and mold and playfully create, sans screen. And that takes a bunch of "stuff," and a place for that stuff to live.

Some call them junk drawers, or craft closets, or art rooms. I call mine a creativity cupboard: an old armoire I painted white and filled with "stuff" with which to artfully create. What I discovered by incorporating it into my main living space is that providing a designated and organized spot for all that glitter and tissue paper, and Mod Podge, and glue, which was fully accessible to all who dared to venture in, made us want to venture in. A lot.

Use an old dresser, a few shelves in a guest room closet, a vintage bar

cart, or some cool piece you pick up at a flea market, and then purpose-fully stock it with all the arts and crafts crap you can find. And then visit it often and play along.

Here are some must-includes:

* Pipe cleaners
* Aluminum foil
* Drinking straws
* Toothpicks
* Construction paper, tissue paper, tracing paper
* Toilet paper rolls
* Rubber bands
* Crayons, markers, pencils, and pens
* Scotch tape, washi tape, duct tape, and masking tape
* Popsicle sticks
* All that other stuff you buy at the craft store

Make 'Em Laugh, Make 'Em Laugh, Make 'Em Laugh

Fill a basket on top of your kitchen island, or in a reachable cupboard, with snippets of fun to be whipped out at a moment's notice. I keep all sorts of playful goodies tucked neatly into the middle drawer of the island in my kitchen. I spend loads of time behind that kitchen island, and it's often where homework gets done, snacks get eaten, and "hangry" meltdowns erupt. Your first line of defense against the dark arts is a really good belly laugh. When everyone's had an exhausting day and your kids have elevated their bickering to presidential debate status, pulling out the magic wand of what we call "whackadoodle" can turn that train wreck around right quick. Fifteen minutes of laughing together can turn Voldemort into Harry. Or at the very least, Ron.

Here are a few spells to tuck away for when you need them most:

1. Joke and riddle books
2. Funny "table talk" question cards
3. Goofy temporary tats
4. Emoji stickers and index cards. Have them make up sentences using only the stickers!
5. Washable window markers
6. "Would you rather?" cards
7. A whoopee cushion
8. Never Have I Ever–type cards
9. Clown noses
10. Tongue twisters. You can find them online!
11. Self-adhesive mustaches
12. Mad Libs tablets
13. Groucho Marx glasses

Play in the Front Yard Much More

If you are fortunate enough to have a backyard, then you know the temptation to hide out in your own patch of private, fenced-in bliss, tucked away from those pesky neighbors of yours. Trust me, I love me some seclusion too. But when a suburban neighborhood full of families looks more uninhabited than Jupiter—Houston, we have a problem.

After interviewing Mike Lanza, the author of *Playborhood: Turn Your Neighborhood into a Place for Play*, I got a bee in my bonnet to see if playing more out front for all to see would really make my neighbors join in. Spoiler alert: It did. Instead of always setting up the cornhole game (we're Midwesterners; look it up), or the badminton net, or the Slip'N Slide out back, I began setting it up in the front yard instead. And our yard became a playful kid-magnet. Which I loved.

Also, as a toy and game spokesperson I get TONS of toy samples delivered to my door every week, to test out with my family. Now, instead of testing the sidewalk art materials, and Nerf Blasters and flying discs in the backyard, I bring them out front in hopes of attracting a crowd. People bond through playful experiences in the most authentic way possible. What better way to really get to know and appreciate your neighbors, and random people passing by, than by offering them a turn at the Stomp Rocket?

Run Away from Home

Get yourself a secret-ish getaway, or simply fake it till you make it. Six years ago my husband and I invested in a lake cottage in Southwest Michigan, about an hour and a half from where we live on the North Shore of Chicago.

With both of us in jobs that require a significant amount of time connected to screens, deadlines, audiences, and social media platforms, we yearned for a place in which to fully disconnect, in order to really re-connect. Our cottage has no Internet access, television, or landline, and we strictly limit cell phone use and social sharing while we're there—for our kids and ourselves. Instead of tech, we invested in hands-on playfulness for the cottage: a trampoline, a shuffleboard table, a vintage arcade game, a zipline, a big round six-seater card table, a record player, and enough games to slay screen envy for good. It has been one of the very best things we've ever done for our family, and I'd say it's our most favorite place to be.

I realize that not everyone has the privilege of a vacation home and the ability to run away to a second location in order to spend quality time with the ones they love most. But I believe there are ways to duplicate the character we've created in our own hideaway in the woods.

How about telling everyone you know that you're "going away for the weekend" and then secretly cocooning yourselves like hermits in your own house, away from the crowd? This might sound a little liar-y, but it's actually a whole lot of brilliance. Once your friends and family think you'll be away and "off the grid," confiscate everyone's devices for a day or two, don't answer the phone (unless it's an emergency), and then escape to the secret hideout of your own four walls. Even for one day, go device-free and introduce your kids to some of the beloved ways you used to get playful when you were a kid. Like . . .

1. Kick the can
2. Shrinky Dinks
3. Classic neighborhood games like flashlight tag or ghost in the graveyard
4. Camp out in sleeping bags on the living room floor.
5. Fake a power outage, light hordes of candles, and tell spooky or funny stories with a flashlight under your chin.
6. Sing-along Disney movie marathons with endless popcorn and a movie candy bar
7. Backyard campout complete with a tent, fire pit, campfire songs, and s'mores
8. Charades. Introduce this old-school goodness to your kids if you haven't.
9. Horse, pig, and knockout variations of basketball. All you need is a hoop and a ball.
10. Base runner. This became my boys' favorite backyard game. My husband and I stand on bases across from each other, fifteen to twenty feet apart, with baseball gloves and a ball. The object of the game is

for the base runners (our boys) to run back and forth between us, while my husband and I throw the ball to each other and try not to get tagged "out."

Creating a connective family "getaway" without a place to actually get away involves a dash of witness protection program mixed with a massive scoop of creativity. Process over product, people.

Purchasing a Little Playfulness

Once you begin adding pops of playfulness about your home, you'll want to know where to find your next hit of whimsy. I'm not proposing that you fill your home with unnecessary stuff. Not even a little bit.

Remember, cluttered chaos does not make a well-played home. But when the opportunity arises to select something new for your home, whether it's a couch, desk, blender, or throw pillow, why not consider something that elicits a playful reaction? COLOR and fun is the new black. But not EVERYTHING needs to be playful and cheeky. You're not after the Willy Wonka vibe here.

What you are after are snippets of Seussian style that will remind you to take a pause for playfulness within your day-to-day, autopilot, household routine.

Here are a few of my favorite "things":

* My white ceramic stag head in the kitchen with tree-branch antlers that I hang playful stuff on to match the season

* My gold-painted powder room with gold frames hung all over the walls that house our family's artwork, mixed with pieces bought on our world travels

* My Tiffany blue, velvety couch splattered with playful throw pillows. Gosh, am I a sucker for a playful throw pillow (cue husband shaking head here).

* Among my faves is my furry sheep-hair pillow from our trip to Iceland and one that says "Imagine." We really don't use our imaginations enough. This pillow acts as a fluffy reminder.

* My candy bar cart. Ever since the dawn of *Mad Men*, I had been on the hunt for a snazzy mid-century bar cart. Because martinis. When I found a cool silver number in HomeGoods for 125 bucks I snagged it right quick and brought it home. But after my husband (ever the voice of reason) suggested that laying out and serving up a plethora of alcohol, almost literally on a silver platter, with a seventeen-year-old in the house might not be the best parenting choice, I decided to make it a candy bar instead. And it's become one of the best additions to my mom movie nights. I try to stock it with vintage candy. And Skittles. The brain food that helped me write a lot of this book.

* The golden turtle that sits on my coffee table. Because she's a badass and reminds me to slow down and not to take anything too seriously.

What are the most playful places and decorative pieces scattered around your house? If you aren't sure, take a moment to walk through your home and write down what strikes playfulness in your heart and soul.

Here, take a moment to record what you find:

1. _____

2. _____

3. _____

4. _____

5. _____

Well Played

If you can't find at least five things in your home that speak to your playful spirit, you've got some fun work to do. It's for the greater good of creating a well-played home. Treat thyself!

Need a smidge of imaginative inspiration for adding more pops of playful whimsy to your own crib? (Do the cool people still say "crib"?)

Anyway, if ya do, I got you.

Here are some of the best spots to score playful design pieces for your home:

* CB2
* IKEA
* Bezar.com
* HomeGoods
* T.J.Maxx
* Marshalls
* West Elm
* eBay
* Antiques stores and vintage toy shops
* Flea markets
* The Land of Nod
* Etsy
* Jellio
* Marimekko
* Fatboy
* Stokke
* Dot & Bo
* AllModern
* Dick Blick Art Materials. This one is like a candy store for me!

It doesn't take a big renovation or expensive design elements to make your home a well-played home. Trust me, those design bloggers and their Instagram feeds full of stunningly playful rooms that look too good to be true . . . yeah, they *are* actually too good to be true! The goal here is not design-blog perfection. The goal is a playfully designed space that encourages all who enter to let their playful spirit run free now and again.

The art of assembling a well-played home is anchored in truth and authenticity, rigged up with ropes of connection and joy, and set sail by a simple, yet very intentional, shift in perspective. A shift from product to process, good impressions to free expression, perfection to playfulness.

"It's a happy talent to know how to play"

- RALPH WALDO EMERSON

Play with your Family

*T*his Emerson quote is one of my favorite go-to, stick-on-the-fridge sayings. I first saw it etched on a wooden plaque hanging on the wall of a gift shop in the Northwoods of Wisconsin many years ago. And these nine words zinged me. Hard. I fell in love with the quote not only because it's all about play, although that was quickly becoming my "niche" in the blogging world at the time. It was also because I loved and still love the adjective-noun combo platter of "happy talent" used to describe what it is to get fully lost in a playful moment. It's a talent. And it's a happy one.

Children are instant pros when it comes to their talent for playfulness. They need little if any instruction on how it works or when to apply its principles, and they never say no to extra hours of practice. Play is always a child's first mode of attack for new experiences, natural curiosities, or unfamiliar territory. It's what their spirits simply long to do. I remember as a young girl setting up elaborate pretend classrooms in my bedroom where I taught my stuffed animal students everything from math and science to music and modern dance. The world outside of my bedroom door did not exist as I became fully lost in my own imagination. Those dolls and bears and Cabbage Patch Kids were my first pupils (and they were always so quiet and well behaved). I'm fairly certain that those hours and hours spent teaching my imaginary classroom of scribes made standing up in front of a real one as an elementary level teacher feel like coming home.

The only addition I might make to Emerson's charming words is that play is also a natural talent, maybe even a supernatural one. A delightful talent we all possess. But there's a quirky little catch. While we're all born with the beautiful joy-producing talent of playfulness, like any other talent, you can appear to lose it if ya don't use it. I slowly started losing my own wonderfully playful spirit after having my second child, becoming anxious and exhausted, focusing on simply keeping my life fully under "control." That five-year span of my life nearly did me in. It was only after consciously shifting my parenting perspective from one of constant order, predictability, and perfection to one of flexible structure, natural surprise, and the beauty of imperfection that I was able to relax into the joy of raising my kids and pursuing my own playful interests. Control is a major play killer.

The awesome news is that if you are blessed to have children in your life, you've been given the gift of what I like to call "permanent play pimps"! And they are there to remind you every darn day that this happy talent still dwells just below your to-do-list-obsessed, all-grown-up facade.

You can try and run from your adorable little play monsters, but you cannot hide. And if you do hide, they'll totally seek and find you.

Whether you are home with your kids all day or work outside of the home (I refuse to use the terms "stay-at-home," "full-time/part-time" or "working mom," because we're all parents, full-time, and we all work, hard), we all want to make the most of the moments we have together as a family. And the best moments are usually the most playful ones.

When my boys were small and I was home 24/7, I thought I played with my kids ALL. THE. TIME. But as I began looking more closely into what it meant to truly play, I quickly realized that what I was doing was setting up and managing THEIR play. I was skilled at creating playful, creative, and enriching activities for them and then sitting back and admiring my good-mom-ness. But our children long for more than play agents who get them playing gigs and then take twenty percent of the credit. They long to see us join the fun and games as well. And so do our own inner eight-year-olds. What our kids really want is to see us get wasted on a mocktail of utter joy and childlike giddiness once in a while too. Have you ever hopped up onto a trampoline with your kids and acted like an over-caffeinated five-year-old, totally "owned" them in a family Nerf Blaster battle, or had an impromptu jam session with instruments you can all barely play? I have. And here's the thing: Once your kids see that kind of full-on, lost-in-Neverland goodness coming out of one of their parents, a look of "Good heavens . . . you're one of US!" flashes across their faces, and it's ON like Donkey Kong. They'll suddenly know what you're really capable of when you forget about "adulting" every now and again. And then because they've had a sweet taste of it, your little minions will be there in a flash to help you conjure up your playful spirit when you need it most. That's good stuff right there.

Listen: This book is not about adding more to-dos to your list or guilt to your trip. I'm not telling you to play more with your kids because it makes you a better, more awesome parent. I'm assuring you that by simply adding more purposeful acts of playfulness to your everyday life, there's a happy talent you'll rediscover—a talent you've had inside of you all along, and one that has the power to make your busy, responsibility-filled life a whole lot more fun, happy, and reconnected to the folks who mean the most to you. And we all want that, right?

Preproducing the Playfulness

*L*et's all take a beat, a very purposeful beat in our claustrophobic days to conduct a bit of playful preproduction, shall we?

My husband is a TV producer, and after watching him at his job for the past twenty-five years I've learned a few very important and consistent truths. One is that preproduction is pretty much everything.

When I started doing *Today* show segments four years ago I learned very swiftly that for every three-minute segment I did, there were at least five hours of preproduction work that needed to happen before the cameras started rolling, to make those three minutes seem effortless. "Prepro," as we say in the business, is the stuff that goes on behind the scenes. All the preparation and work the audience never sees, but benefits from greatly. Preproduction helps just as much when producing playful moments with your kiddos as it does when trying to pull off a live segment on national TV.

Even in the seemingly spontaneous bits of life, a smidge of smart planning is often what allows us to be happily engulfed by a present moment. Don't get me wrong, I LOVE spontaneity! The element of surprise, the risky thrill of the unplanned, and the spur-of-the-moment of it all are important ingredients in the recipe for a more playful life. But for most of us, with packed schedules, multitasks collectively hollering at us, and too-short days that seem to begin and end in a flurry of activity, the idea of families spontaneously skipping into an episode of unabashed playfulness is usually left for shows on the Disney Channel.

But don't turn the channel! If living a more joyous, playful, creative, and connected life is something you're after, there are ways to preproduce those playful moments and trick your audience into thinking you "woke up like this."

I should tell you that I am one of the world's best day-crammers ever. Most mornings I can be found sipping my morning coffee, making to-do lists the size of Texas, and filling in each and every waking moment. Including potty breaks. While I adore the "Let's jump in the pool with our clothes on" or "Who wants to dance till two A.M.?" moments, alternatively I can be a slightly anxious person, who takes forever to fall asleep due to Chicken Little syndrome, just waiting for the sky to come on down, who's also in love with lists and predictability. I'm a walking dichotomy . . . and a joy to live with (no, really . . . I am).

I understand that the notion of "planning" for a spontaneous moment may sound a little counterintuitive. But until we all break the busy-equals-better habit, we're going to need some practice in leaving some intentional S P A C E for that unstructured, "last-minute," playful magic to unfold.

Stopping the constant motion of our lives and considering ways to add more pure playfulness into our daily grinds puts us way ahead of the game. I recently posted on Facebook that I wanted to be better at "leaving space for the spontaneous," and a friend commented that the mere thought of not having her planner filled in and scheduled gave her a mild case of the shakes. So I suggested that she actually schedule time for playfulness to pop on by, "spontaneously." Remember, it's your neighborhood of make-believe; you get to be Queen Sara and make up the rules.

If you want more fun and frivolity in your everyday, PLAN FOR IT.

Step one is to slow down for a minute, take a beat, and go ahead and try your hand at a little playful preproduction.

I've got a few tricks for you.

"Play Crates"

When I was teaching elementary school I often created thematic bins of play-based learning activities we called "centers" or "stations." Do they still do centers in elementary classrooms? I hope so, because guess what? Kids flipping LOVE centers, or what I now call "play crates." Play crates are simply homemade bins or boxes of fun, constructed around a playful theme. There is something unicorn-magical about having a box full of play-based, thematic goodies to dive into, matched up with a simple prompt for playfulness. It's MAG-I-CAL, I tell you.

These make-ahead fun-bombs take very little time to assemble but are like a shot of good tequila when no one is feeling very playful or creative, and the walls of your home begin to feel like they're closing in on you (I'm looking at *you*, Chicago winters and really every dang over-scheduled night with kids) . . . can I get an amen!?

When making your own play crates, you'll want to include activities that your younguns can do independently, plus some stuff that you're secretly stoked to do along with them. Remember our earlier chat about the awesome benefits of playtime for YOU? Yeah, I was serious about that. It's cool to be self-serving when it comes to play.

Hit up your local Michaels craft store or whatever big crafty place you have in your 'hood, and choose items that play well together to create a themed experience. Pack the materials into the play-crate containers of

your choice, pop them on a shelf, and BAM! Instant playfulness when you'll need it most. The possibilities are endless. You're going to have a good time putting these together, I promise.

Martha Stewart and I have just about one thing in common. Our initials. Please know that I am missing the perfectly-crafty-in-every-way DNA possessed by Ms. Stewart. I am no expert in the "maker" movement, and most of the stuff on Pinterest scares the hell out of me. Therefore, when my boys were little, I cheated my way through the craft store as much as possible. I gathered fun ideas for my play crates from teacher resource books, favorite online sources, and craft store idea sheets, as well as tricks I picked up from my days teaching elementary and preschool children and adapted for my own.

One of my boys' favorite play crates was something we called the "animal hospital." (No real animals were harmed in the making of this crate.) Inside a computer-paper-size box was everything my little dudes needed to diagnose, stitch, bandage, mend up, and take care of all the peculiar ailments of their stuffed animals and action figures. Our attic

playroom would instantly turn into a pediatric ward for the pretend, with rows of blanket "beds" holding everything from Buzz Lightyear and his broken wing to G.I. Joe nursing a mean concussion to a Care Bear with a wicked case of the stomach flu. And when I tell you my boys spent hours in the land of make-believe playing doctor and triaging all of toyland, I'm talking HOURS.

Play-Crate Houses

Use whatever you've got handy to house your play crates. It doesn't have to be a "crate," I just like how that name nearly rhymes. I am a sucker for rhyming and awesome accurate alliteration, so know that too as you read this book.

Here are some play crate containers I think are simply swell (see what I did there?):

* Gallon-size zip-top bags
* Sturdy shoe boxes
* Pringles cans
* Tennis ball cans
* Plastic takeout food containers (well washed)
* Photo boxes
* Under-the-bed plastic bins with lids

* Plastic zipper pouches you get with bedsheet and comforter sets

* Small wooden crates from the craft store

The best part of the play crate is that it shows up when they least expect it, proceeds to be the life of the party, and then disappears for a few weeks or months, making them long for its return. Not awesome qualities in a significant other, but super-awesome attributes in a "We're bored!" parenting pinch. Trust me on this: Play crates are totally worth the preproduction.

Let's get this preproduction party started!

Here's a list of simple play crate ideas you can whip up in a weekend:

FOIL AND SCOTCH TAPE SCULPTURES

* Rolls of inexpensive aluminum foil
* Various kinds of tape (colorful washi tape, Scotch tape, duct tape)
* Play prompts written on note cards, like "Create a new kind of dinosaur," "Construct a shiny new house for your fairies," "Build a skyscraper," or "Make your favorite zoo animal"

DIY PUPPETS

. . . Because Puppets Are Just Weird Enough to Be Delightful

* Brown or colored paper lunch bags
* Old, clean socks
* Stickers
* Googly eyes

* Various kinds of tape
* Glue sticks
* Yarn, twine, or raffia
* Ribbon scraps
* Cloth remnants
* Markers or crayons

POPSICLE STICK STRUCTURES

* Popsicle sticks
* Tongue depressors
* Toothpicks
* Glue or a mini hot glue gun
* Small cardboard base
* Your stellar architectural skills

HOMEMADE SNOW GLOBES

See page 92 for directions for making your homemade snow globes.

* Baby food jars
* Small plastic animals, action figures, or other small figurines to glue to the lid
* Artificial snow or white glitter
* Small bottle of glycerin (found at the drugstore)

BUBBLE-PALOOZA

. . . Because You Can't Blow Bubbles and Be Grumpy at the Same Time

* A variety of different bubble wands in different sizes and shapes

* Premade bubble soap or ingredients to make your own "Biggest Bubble Ever Solution"
* Pie pans for the bubble fluid
* Have your kids play with this crate in the bathtub!

TISSUE PAPER MOSAICS

* Large pieces of construction paper
* Assortment of brightly colored tissue paper, cut into two-by-two-inch squares
* Paste or glue sticks
* Prompts, like "Look outside your window and create a still life of what you see, using the stuff in this box"

The possibilities are seriously endless when it comes to the kinds of play crates you can create. It's also fun to get your kids in on the action of producing them with you. Kids are always more invested and interested in just about anything if they help to create it. It's totally okay if they know what's coming down the road, and it doesn't lessen the excitement on the day you decide to pull one out to play. Let the interests of your kids be your guide. Then scour craft books, parenting magazines, and online sources like Pinterest.

I'm a little bitter that I didn't have the magnificent online bulletin board system known as Pinterest back when my boys were little, but you do, so use it, people! It's like getting every creative, playful, crafty, fun idea known to man in one swift click. If you've never gone on a playdate with Little Miss Pinterest, you should be aware that while she's AMAZING, she's also a real tease. So let me give you a few quick tips for navigating her overwhelming good looks and mind-numbing perfectionism . . . 'cause that chick can take you down.

Pinterest: Check Yourself Before You Wreck Yourself

1. **NEVER ARRIVE EMPTY-HANDED.** Before you even double-click on Pinterest's front door, make a list of what you're looking for and what you hope to gain from the relationship. Or it will be like skipping into a Target "just to see if there is anything you might need" (hello, two hours and three hundred dollars later with nothing for dinner). Enter with an idea of what you want, and give yourself a time limit for your visit.

2. **THE SEARCH BOX IS LIKE YOUR ADDICTION SPONSOR.** Use her to help keep you on the wagon. Guard yourself against aimlessly barhopping from board to board. Again, it can be the time-suck of the century and leave you with a "What just happened to the last two hours?" hangover. If you're there to find playful activities for you and your fam, go straight to the search bar upon arrival and pop in search words like "play, family activities, indoor fun, rainy-day fun, creative play, etc." Then make your pin boards from there. Focused use of the search bar will keep you sober.

3. **PIN WITH PURPOSE.** If you've never "pinned" ideas on Pinterest.com, first, how's that rock you've been living under? And second, Pinterest is basically a digital bulletin board system that allows you to create multiple bulletin boards with images and ideas on everything from remodeling a kitchen, fall fashion trends, and winter recipes to party ideas and every DIY project you could ever imagine or would never have dreamed of. It's

brilliant for finding quick and beautiful lifestyle inspiration. The flip side is that it can be tsunami-like . . . just way too much of a good thing. I've found it's less intimidating to pin ideas on one board at a time instead of hunting and gathering for all of your boards at once. By creating very specific boards for various topics like "rainy-day fun," "playful DIYs," "best new toys and games for summer," etc., it helps you know right where to look when you need a quick idea on a particular topic.

If you're looking for summer fun inspiration, work on just that board for a set amount of time instead of hopping back and forth from board to board.

....

4. **DON'T PIN ALONE.** Bring your kids along on your Pinterest exploration! They love looking at all of the fun ideas and helping to pick the ones that look the most appealing to them. Decide upon the ideas and activities you'd really love to try, and make a play board together. You can create "private" play boards on Pinterest, too, for the times when you just want to surprise their socks off.

....

5. **BEWARE OF THE COMPARE** . . . it will spoil the whole darn thing. "Process over product" is your mantra. There are whole websites filled with "Pinterest fails," showing images documenting various ways people have totally botched a beautiful idea they found on the Pinterest site. There are hundreds of posts for a reason. I find the sites kind of hilarious, but remember, in the game of creativity and playfulness, as in many things in life, comparison is the thief of joy. And joy is what we're after here.

Now go show Pinterest who's the boss lady.

Good luck, and Godspeed.

Marie Lebaron, author and creator of MakeAndTakes.com

1. Crafting keeps me young. I get to be silly and creative, using my imagination to continue exploring and discovering new things. I'm always learning and growing—that doesn't change when you become an adult.

2. Arts and crafts as an outlet. One of the reasons I craft as an adult is to go to my happy place. While I'm crafting, I have time to think and process my day. As I paint, draw, or crochet, I'm able to take a little time out for myself and pause the world, being quiet and simply thinking.

3. Leading by example. My children all have the creative bug, and I know it's because they see their mom crafting too. They see that I take time out to crochet or doodle, and I know it inspires them to do the same. When kids see adults participating, they know that they can do it too. It can help prompt kids into being crafty and encourage their creative side.

4. Evaluate my kids. As I craft with my kids, I'm able to participate in their process. I get to watch how they work: if they problem solve, how they transition, if they need support cutting or drawing, and their dialogue. There are some pretty fun conversations going on during the arts and crafts time. You can learn so much from crafting with your kids.

5. Craft to simply have more fun. There's so much fun exploration with arts and crafts, and it's so necessary to the joy of life. Whether you're playing with play dough, watercolor, or yarn, it's just so fun to play, especially crafting with your kids!

TIE-DYE CRAYONS

What You'll Need

* Crayons (try gathering up the broken ones in the bottom of your art box)
* Silicone baking molds in fun shapes like letters or animals
* An oven

Directions

1. Kids can help with these first two steps. Make sure all paper is removed from the crayon pieces.

2. Preheat the oven to 230°F. Fill the silicone baking mold with broken crayon pieces, using a mix of colors in each mold for a tie-dyed effect.

3. Bake the crayons for 15 minutes. Make sure to let the crayons cool before giving them to little hands.

4. Make these crayons for parties, gifts, or just for fun on a rainy day!

Make a Family PLAYlist

On my website, MeredithPlays.com, we provide readers with a template for a "Family PLAYlist," to help too-busy-to-play families take a moment to map out ways they want to play together for the coming week, month, season, or year. Again . . . PREPRODUCTION, people! Never underestimate it.

When mapping out your family's playlist, try to include both big adventures and experiences that take purposeful preproduction and planning, as well as simple play breaks that cost next to nothing and can be done at a moment's notice.

Documenting your playful intentions matters. When we take a moment to write down and schedule the things that are important to us, we are much more likely to actually DO the stuff we talk, talk, talk about.

Y'all might not get to every last thing on your playlists, and honestly that's not even the point. It's seeing that fun-filled list hanging up on your fridge or magnetic master calendar every day that becomes a happy reminder that you want more splashes of playful family connection stirred into your swirling cocktail of life.

It should be noted that there are different columns on this Family PLAYlist, which encourages you to add more playfulness throughout the different bits of your life. Remember, super-parents of the world, it is just as important to plan pops of playtime with your own pals, with your mate, and all by yourself. Do that, will ya!?

My Playlist

Playground (My Home)

1.

2.

3.

4.

5.

With Family

1.

2.

3.

4.

5.

MAKING ROOM FOR PURPOSEFUL ACTS OF PLAYFULNESS THIS YEAR

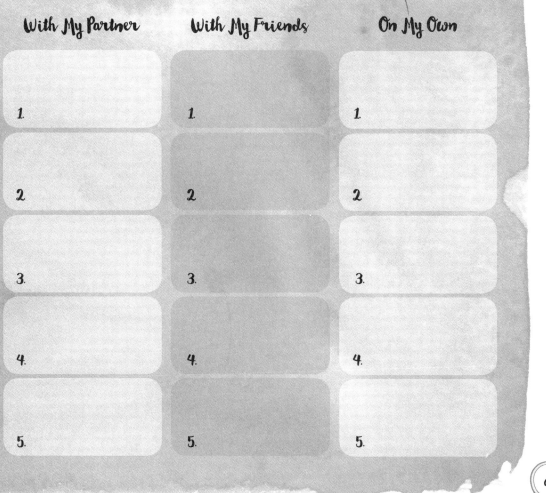

With My Partner

1.

2.

3.

4.

5.

With My Friends

1.

2.

3.

4.

5.

On My Own

1.

2.

3.

4.

5.

A peek at some of our own family PLAYlist activities:

* "Make an igloo in the backyard and have lunch inside." We've had to make friends with the LONG Chicago winter. It's play, or die. If you live in a place where it snows and stays cold for weeks and months on end, you'll find that constructing a backyard igloo, using snow-brick makers, provides days and days of outside fun. It's been one of my boys' favorite places to play and hang out during our many months of ice-age weather in Chicago.

* "Set up a hot cocoa bar with tons of toppings, make a pillow and blanket nest, and watch *Elf*," our very favorite Christmas movie. We kick it up a notch by playing a drinking game using mini marshmallow and hot chocolate "shots" and a list of movie quotes to listen for throughout the flick. (Add a splash of Baileys to yours, and everyone's a winner!)

* "Construct a homemade slip-and-slide down the grassy hill at the lake cottage."

* "Have a pillow fight with Mom and Dad's good down pillows, set to the soundtrack from *Despicable Me*."

* "Plan a ski trip to a place we've never been before."

* "Dance a little more. Every day. Just pump up the jams and DANCE."

* "Buy or borrow a karaoke machine and have a sing-off on New Year's Eve."

* "Take a cooking class with Maxwell."

* "Get out the five million Nerf Blasters we own and have a full-on parents vs. kids showdown at the basement corral."

* "Buy some spray paint and a big white canvas and explore the art of graffiti, in the backyard."

* "Hold a kite-flying contest on the beach."

* "Invite couples over to play *Hollywood Game Night*."

* "Play Four Square and base runner in the backyard."

* "Hop on your bike once a week, without the kids and with no agenda, and go where your soul leads you."

* "Host a Mom Movie Night to celebrate back-to-school, featuring the movie *Sixteen Candles*."

Remember, setting an intention to incorporate pops of playfulness into our busy lives provides us with a visual reminder of the game-changing joy to be found in strapping on our fun selves, disconnecting from the "busy," and reconnecting with the folks who matter most to us: one another.

"I SPY" ON-THE-GO BAGS

What You'll Need

* Up to 25 small items like buttons, beads, and tiny toys
* Camera
* White paper
* Pencil pouch with transparent front (the kind that fit in 3-ring binders)
* 6 inches of ribbon
* Needle and thread
* 8 ounces poly pellets, found at most hobby stores (for more of a challenge, use colored beads of different sizes)
* Hot glue gun

Directions

1. Lay all of your small items out on a white piece of paper and take a photograph of them all together. Print this photo (5 x 7 is good). On the back side of the photo, write or type a list of the items. Laminating this photo will help it last longer.

2. Stitch one end of your ribbon onto the top of your picture card. Stitch the other end of the ribbon to the pencil pouch so the two will stick together!

3. Put your small items and poly pellets into the pouch and zip it up.

4. Use the hot glue gun to cover the zipper teeth and keep everything inside. You can also sew the zipper pull to the pouch to be extra careful that it won't come unzipped.

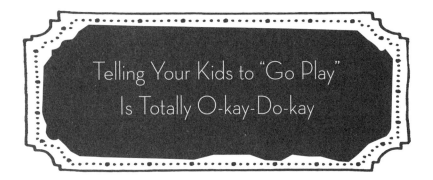

Telling Your Kids to "Go Play"
Is Totally O-kay-Do-kay

Parental PSA

There is no guilt or resentment or misery allowed in play!

Open-ended, independent play is fabulous for our kids. Play is their work, and sometimes they need to do it all alone. Of course, it's also fantastic when we fully engage in playful experiences along with them. There's proven mental, physical, and emotional goodness that shows up when we invite more playfulness into our parenting. But here's the thing. What's totally not fantastic for anyone involved is when we feel like sticking hot forks in our eyeballs because we JUST CAN'T MAKE ANOTHER MATCHBOX CAR NOISE, or put one more bright pink Barbie shoe onto that girl's uncooperative little feet. You can only fake enjoyment for so long, and your kids totally know when you're phoning it in, and loathing every minute of it.

Kids actually need the opportunity to play alone and guide their own imaginations, especially when we can't be fully present or just aren't picking up what they're playfully putting down. Instead of being able to separate our love for them from our aversion for the finger paints, what they feel is "You're completely miserable being with ME." So, on the days you just can't bring yourself to be a Ninja Turtle or Elsa from *Frozen* ONE. MORE. TIME . . . let it go! And joyfully set them up with some independent play. Then go have a shot of espresso and try again later.

Playful Ways to Kick Open the Doors of Communication with Your Kids

When our kids are little they long to tell us EVERYTHING . . . all day long, and over and over and over, to share their crazy trains of thought and personal nuggets of truth that show us who they are and who they are becoming. I'd like to tell you that every time my young sons told me one of their stories about the mayhem going down with Thomas the Tank Engine and his band of train mates, or how G.I. Joe planned to rescue one of his fellow soldiers, or everything that was happening in their personal lands of make-believe, I listened intently. Eyes locked on theirs, super engaged, fully attentive. But then you'd call bullsh*t on me and close this book right now and donate it to the library.

I think it's safe to say that we all know how important it is to listen to and interact with the folks in our immediate family on a regular basis. Open, inviting, free-flowing communication is the gateway to true connection with our kids and partners. It's also a primary ingredient in the whole healthy parent/child relationship thing. And I'm pretty sure we are all doing the gosh-darn best we can to be fully "present" with our people, amid filled-up lives of real stuff that needs to get done. It's harder than it has ever been to fully focus on one thing at a time. But it's also more important than it's ever been, given the constant barrage of very influential external voices and threads and hashtags and Snapchats and YouTube-ery clambering for our attention.

I always discover a whole lot more about someone (especially my own kids) when we're engaged in some type of playful experience. A connected and joyful relationship with your children as they make their way along the path to adulthood requires intention, attention, and action. That shizzle doesn't just "happen." Especially in our current state of mass distraction.

My sons go much "deeper" with me and are much more willing to let me in on what's happening inside when we're engaged in an activity like playing catch with a football, shooting hoops, battling it out on a Ping-Pong table, jumping on the trampoline, or making something crafty and fun. Play has this uncanny way of revealing someone's true spirit, releasing inhibitions and ego to allow what's been hidden to make its way out. Play reveals how someone reacts to new experiences, frustrations, collaboration, and allows for the naked freedom to forget others' judgment and be who they really are.

So let's get this playful communication party started, shall we? The following ideas are yours to mess with as you please. I offer them up as a launchpad for your own creativity and interpretation. They've been useful in bringing my brood together in a playful and fun way, and I hope they do the same for you.

GLOW-IN-THE-DARK BOWLING

What You'll Need

* Glow sticks
* Tall clear empty plastic bottles
* Hamster ball to make a glow-in-the-dark bowling ball

Directions

1. Activate 1 or 2 glow sticks and place them in a bottle. You can fill the bottles with some water to keep them upright. Put lids back on the bottles.

....

2. Tape the desired number of glow sticks to the inside of the hamster ball, close, and secure with tape to make a glow-in-the-dark bowling ball. Time to play!

Write All Over Your Dinner Table

Every so often I'll grab my roll of inexpensive butcher paper or chalkboard paper and use it as an interactive table runner down the center of my dining room table or kitchen island. I don't save it for special occasions or birthday parties; I save it for random Wednesday nights or when people are looking grumpy and over one another. I also pop a batch of fresh washable markers or colored chalk in a pretty vase in the middle of the table.

I encourage (but not demand . . . kids run from demand) that we use this blank space to jot down "jokes of the day," inspiring quotes, riddles, trivia questions, or random doodles, as everyone sees fit. "The table runner of awesome" becomes a fun dinner conversation piece and a reminder to stop and take a doodle break now and again. I like to encourage guests to add to the runner as well. Leave it up for a couple of weeks and see how fun-filled-in it becomes.

This collaborative runner is also a playful addition to family gatherings over the holidays or as part of big ol' get-togethers. It's just fun to scribble on the table, and it helps encourage folks to abandon their smartphones and interact and talk with one another.

THE NO-MESS MURAL

What You'll Need

* Roll of clear contact paper (the kind used for shelf lining)
* Painter's tape
* Odds and ends from your kids' craft box: foam shapes, mini pom-poms, random stickers, buttons, ribbon scraps, fun-shaped confetti, etc.

Directions

1. Cut a long length of contact paper to fit your wall. Make it as long as possible.

2. Remove the backing so that the sticky side is face-up.

3. Tape the length of paper onto your wall at kid height, so that the sticky side faces you.

4. Place the crafty odds and ends into the compartments of a muffin tin or on a tray.

5. Let your toddlers and preschoolers have a ball creating a 3-D mural by simply pressing the craft goodies onto the sticky paper.

6. To preserve their artistic masterpiece, simply place a slightly larger piece of clear contact paper over the top and press to seal.

Throw Something at Your Children

I have some of the very best connection sessions with my boys when we are engaged in throwing or hitting something at one another. Baseballs, footballs, Frisbees, beach balls, tennis balls, Ping-Pong balls, anything that can be tossed back and forth or safely launched at one another. I don't think this is limited to boys, and I have no idea why it happens, but the act of playing catch opens up kids like a package on Christmas morning, often all at once and very willingly.

I'm just going to chalk it up to Plato knowing what he was talking about, again. You want your older kids to spill their guts? Whip something at them. And make them whip it back.

Write All Over Those Nice Clean Windows Too!

Grab a handful of thick washable window markers (found at craft, art, and big-box stores), and encourage your kids to go to town on a sliding glass door, large window, or even the mirror in the bathroom. As with the table runner, this clear canvas is an unexpected space for you to pose your own open-ended, creative questions or inspiring quotes as well, which become the perfect catalysts for family chats. It all comes off with a wet paper towel, so chill, Mama, chill.

DOABLE DIY

Here are some easy and fun ways to make playful conversation starters of your own.

1. Buy some white paper napkins, and on the back of each person's, ask an open-ended, creative question. Each person at the table shares their answers. Throw in some silly ones too!

2. Use plastic dessert forks, and with a black Sharpie write the beginning of a riddle on each person's fork handle. Take turns reading the riddle and having the rest of the family try figuring out the answer. (I am acutely competitive when it comes to riddles. I put great effort into coming up with the answer first. My husband thinks it's a real big problem; I think it's my gift to humankind.)

3. Place a pretty bowl in the center of the table filled with what we call "Coke or Pepsi?" questions, like "Cake or pie?" and "Beach or woods?" and "Boxers or briefs?" This is my son Truman's absolute favorite questioning game. In fact, after a thirty-minute, fun-filled round of this game recently, he turned to me and said, "I learned SO much about you today, Mom! Stuff I never would have expected." SCORE!

Let's Give 'Em Something to Talk About

I have spent many a meal trying to get my boys to tell me what they're thinking, describe what they did at school that day, or simply stop making inappropriate body noises. I want our mealtimes to be fun and connective, but also respectful. We have often used sets of conversation-starter questions, like Table Topics or "would you rather" cards, to help add a spark of silliness to mealtimes while focusing discourse and prompting playful banter. Plus we always end up finding out things about one another we never knew.

Inviting Random Pops of Playfulness into Your Life

Living a more well-played life is a choice we get to make every day. Just like being well hydrated, well read, or well nourished, being more well played takes a shift in priority and perspective. And this simple shift has the capability of changing everything for the better, from waiting in a long line at the grocery store, to another sleep-deprived night and day with young children, to a typical Tuesday night at home when everyone's a little restless and poopy. Opportunities to live more PLAY-FULLY present themselves all the time. We just have to get better at recognizing them and then grabbing them by the playground balls.

Here's a slew of simple ways I've tried to add more playfulness into my own days and nights with these miraculous offspring I've produced.

Have a "Sleepover" for You and Your Kid

I was traveling over a weekend for work recently, and when I came home my husband, Jon, told me that my son Truman had tried to find a friend to come over on Saturday and have a sleepover with him, but that everyone was busy. Tru was annoyed and discouraged and starting to melt down. So, instead of battling the bad vibe, Jon suggested that since my older son was also away for the night, the two of them should have a tween boy sleepover together instead. They watched action movies, popped a massive batch of popcorn, played video games, riffed on their guitars, and basically acted like total immature middle-schoolers. If you are going to try this with your own kid, the key is to avoid behaving like a grown-up pretending to have a sleepover with your kid. Instead, act like your kid does when he or she is having a sleepover with one of his or her friends. It's your chance to act your shoe size in the name of "good parenting." Grab that, hard.

SAVE THE KIDS GAME

What You'll Need

* 10 Sour Patch Kids
* Paper plate
* Whipped cream

Directions

1. Put 10 Sour Patch Kids on a paper plate. Cover the candy Kids and the plate with whipped cream.

2. Using no hands and only your mouth, save all 10 pieces of candy from the plate of whipped cream.

3. First player to "rescue" all 10 Kids is the winner!

In Defense of the Dance Party

Have you ever observed skeptical folks on social media commenting about the legitimacy of having dance parties in their kitchens with their kids, being all "whatever, no one really does that and it can't be all that awesome, anyway"? Then I have a secret to tell you . . . DANCE PARTIES IN THE KITCHEN WITH YOUR KIDS ARE REALLY ALL THAT AWESOME! Little kids adore them, and big kids, while trying to look mortifyingly embarrassed for the first ten minutes, usually cannot resist the call of the wild for long, and will eventually jump in to bust a move as well. Make some specific kitchen dance-athon playlists ahead of time so you're ready when the urge to free your backed-up Beyoncé comes calling. Pop music and a tile floor make a playful prune juice cocktail when everything's just a little too tightly bound. We like to do a round-robin music selection on the iPad, where each family member takes turns picking a secret song from our music library as we go. It's fun to be surprised by the next tune. Life is crazy, and sometimes you just need to shake your sillies out and sing into a spatula.

Dance Party Super-Tip!

Buy yourself a battery-operated mini disco ball for your kitchen counter, or if you're feeling extra playful and daring, mount a small one on the ceiling somewhere in your kitchen. Then watch how that blows up your dance parties in the best way possible. (I found one at the party store and had my husband mount it.) You're welcome.

Never Underestimate the Magical Powers of a Well-Built Blanket Fort

If you have never made a "fort" using every blanket, pillow, and sheet in the house, you, my friend, have not completed your childhood.

And if you and your kids have never raided the linen closet together in the name of bedcover castle construction, then you need to impart your worldly blanket-fort-making wisdom and show them how it's done. STAT.

I recognize that making a blanket fort together isn't a novel idea. But how long has it been since you've actually tucked blankets into couch cushions, draped sheets over dining chairs, and piled every pillow in the house up for walls? Then crawled inside your cave of quilts with flashlights and books and crumbly snacks, and your best stuffed buddies, for an all-day play powwow? Really? How long?

Here's the thing: This is the most engaging, least expensive screen-free

activity on the planet. And the return on investment is out of this world. Never mock the magic that lies within a blanket fort's cozy walls. Make them as often as possible, and allow for the takeover of your precious living room without angst. They will all fold back up and retreat into their closets once again, I promise. Make them even when your kids have outgrown them. Especially when your kids have outgrown them.

Give Your Family Calendar a Double Shot of Frivolity!

Looking at our overstocked family calendars can be a one-way ticket to Xanaxville. So much to do . . . so little time! As our kids grow and get involved in all sorts of scheduled activities, mapping out everyone's comings and goings can feel like wrangling a litter of feral cats. We have a GIANT dry-erase calendar hung on a wall in our kitchen where everyone's "stuff" is displayed. My husband has taken it upon himself to erase and redo the calendar each month, and over the last couple of years he's managed to transform those boring squares of busy from something overwhelming and unruly to something approachable and fun. It's all in the way he "introduces" each month ("December is Jingle-Diggity"; "July is Sparkle-Diggity") and how he playfully fills in the blanks. Make your family's calendar go from sucky to super, one colored dry-erase marker at a time. Add jokes and funny art! Make it fun to look at.

Jimmy Fallon's Lip-Synch Contests: Make That Musical Joyride Your Own

If you have yet to witness one of Jimmy Fallon's lip-synch battles on *The Tonight Show*, then I give you full permission to earmark this page, go to YouTube, and give a watch. Go go go!

Okay, now that you get the magnificence that is the lip-synch battle, I implore you to hold one of your own with your kids. Everyone picks one song with which to produce a lip-synch routine performed for the rest of the family. NO ONE EVEN HAS TO BE ABLE TO SING. This is brilliant for kid parties, family gatherings, and on a Friday night in with the kids. Hilarious, playful, ridiculous family fun, presented to you with a big red laugh bow on top. Thanks, Jimmy. We love you.

Stockpile Joke Books and Use Them Often. They Are Grumpy Kids' Kryptonite.

I keep a stash of small riddle and joke books in the top drawer of what I call my tropical kitchen island, for when the natives get restless and we're all ready to begin voting each other off the island.

My family quickly loses their sugar when we're hungry or tired after a long day. And I'm not just talking about the children. I've been known to turn into a raging three-year-old when I'm underfed as well. Lead witch of the "witching hour," this one. Whipping out these collections of funny, and launching into a joke or riddle fest while we're cooking dinner, waiting at a restaurant, on a road trip, or before bedtime, turns mayhem into a marvelous family moment. It doesn't suck to invite a good pre-dinner snack to the comedy show too, let's be honest. You can find fun joke books at the local library, dollar store, or neighborhood bookstore. They're a very good investment piece.

Plan for Adventures, Both Massive and Minute

"Life is either a great adventure or nothing."

—HELEN KELLER

Isn't the word "adventure" simply delightful? It's loaded with mystery and layered in possibility. Whether it's climbing Mount Kilimanjaro, writing a book, traveling to a far-off land, or jumping into a ball pit with your child and letting yourself be smothered in playfulness, it's the "daring" to do it that makes something really adventurous, isn't it?

The thing about being adventurous is that it can also be totally intimidating. Most of us don't have time to eat, pray, love ourselves into true happiness and inner peace. I mean, we have carpool and grocery shopping to do! Perhaps our definition of "adventure" is a little bit all wrong. Even Elizabeth Gilbert, author of *Eat, Pray, Love* talks about the need to go on "mini quests." Simple missions that we can do any old time to add more adventure, discovery, and playfulness to our lives. I kind of love that idea. Adventure is about butterflies dancing in our tummies, exploring uncharted territory, or daring to do something semi-scary or to go get wistfully lost for a while.

Discovering a new bike path and spontaneously following it with wild abandon, stumbling into an unfamiliar museum, or exploring a foreign land are all beautiful adventures. Opportunities to get gone in a purely playful and temerarious experience. Encourage yourself to be swallowed up and consumed by adventure! Practice being right where you are and nowhere else. Fully engulfed in the flames of right now (sans smartphones and social sharing). Be wide open to what lies around every little bend! That's where playfulness reveals itself in all its glory.

Everyday Adventures to Pop onto Your Family's Playlist

* Map out a backyard or city block scavenger hunt. Include prompts like: Look for something round, something beautiful, something funny, something that smells good, etc.

* Hit an unfamiliar neighborhood with your kids and see what you find . . . and whom you meet.

* Go to the grocery store and pick out one or two "mystery items" from the produce section. Figure out what they are and what to do with them, and then make it a part of dinner that night!

* Schedule a visit to a library you've never been to, and explore away! Make sure you explore the grown-up shelves too. When's the last time you allowed yourself the time and space to be fully consumed by all those books?

* Go on an artist hunt through a local art museum. I used to do this with my boys, having them look for special pieces and quirky objects throughout.

* Find a patch of woods, pack a basket of goodies, and have a "teddy bear picnic." Or for older kids, go sans teddies, and bring a REAL camera. You know, the kind with lenses and film? After throwing down a big blanket and eating lunch under the trees, have your kids capture nature shots using an actual shutter speed.

* If you live in or near an urban area, hop on your public transportation with nowhere in particular to go. When my boys were little, they loved riding the train down to the city of Chicago, not because we were going into the city but just because we were riding the train. They felt the same way about the bus, the subway, and the water taxi. Forget the destination, and just enjoy the adventure that is the journey.

My Everyday Adventure Playlist

1.

2.

3.

4.

5.

6.

7.

8.

9.

10.

POOL NOODLE RACE TRACK

What You'll Need

* Serrated or electric knife
* Foam pool noodle
* Toothpicks
* Needlenose pliers
* Cardstock
* Scissors and glue
* Racing items like Matchbox cars or marbles

Directions

1. Use the knife to cut the foam noodle into two pieces the long way, then lay the pieces side by side on the ground, cut-sides up.

2. Insert toothpicks into the sides of the foam noodles so they pierce each piece, connecting them. Use as many as you need to keep the two noodles connected.

3. Using the needlenose pliers, clip the ends of the toothpicks so they're flush with the noodles and won't block your matchbox cars from racing down the track.

4. Use your cardstock and toothpicks to create flags and banners to decorate your track. To make things extra on-theme, try picking up some race track stickers from the craft store.

5. To play, prop the noodles up on a chair or other surface, start your engines, and let 'em go!

MASON JAR SNOW GLOBES

What You'll Need

* Metallic or colorful spray paint
* Mini décor, like bottlebrush trees and toy animals
* Mason jars (any size or shape)
* Glue gun and glue sticks
* White glitter or craft "snow"
* Small bottle of glycerin, for filling the snow globe

Directions

1. Spray paint your mini décor and your mason jar lids and rings to best express the theme for your snow globe.

2. Use your glue gun to secure the miniatures to the inside of the jar lid to create your scene.

3. Add a dab of glue along the inside of the lid ring. Place the decorated lid inside the glued ring and secure.

4. Sprinkle a tablespoon or more of glitter or snow inside the jar. Fill the jar with glycerin, leaving ¼ inch at the top, then screw the finished lid onto the snow-filled mason jar.

Shake Things Up!

Monotony and routine can be major play poachers. Feeling like I'm living the reality-show version of the movie *Groundhog Day* can be a very real thing for me, especially during the winter months here in the Midwest . . . have I mentioned our long, cold, gray winters? I also remember some seemingly endless days at home caring for two small children and feeling like many of them were the same exact lineup of eat, sleep, poop, cry; eat, sleep, poop, cry. And that was just me. I beseech you, do not save all of your fun and games for the weekend! There are only four of them every month, for Pete's sake. Instead, pick a random Monday or Wednesday, and do something completely out of the ordinary. Like totally whackadoodle. We do a little something called "More Fun Mondays." 'Cause Monday has a lot of haters, have you noticed? Again, these pops of playfulness do not need to be epic or mighty. They simply need to shake up your day in some sort of playful way.

Here are a few to inspire you:

* Make a homemade birthday cake, decorate it, blow out the candles, and eat it for dessert, even if it's no one's birthday. Because it's someone's birthday, somewhere, every day, whether you know that person or not.
* Do movie night on a Monday night instead of always on Friday or Saturday.
* Throw down a tablecloth and some pillows and have a dinner picnic UNDER the dining room table.
* Let your kids be your stylists and decide what YOU are going to wear one day. Just roll with it and have fun! Saturday or Sunday, or a day you've been quarantined, might be best for this activity.

* That whole disco-ball dance party in the kitchen thing I mentioned earlier. Yeah, do THAT! At breakfast.
* Make one kid at a time the total BOSS for the day. They pick what you do, where you eat, what stories to read, and who takes out the trash and feeds the dog. It's one day! Hand over the helicopter, parents. Let the crew fly for once.

Go Totally Retro on Your New-Millennium Minions

Take the time to teach your kids the retro games you loved so much as a youngun. Ain't no school like the old school.

We all have a few precious games or activities from our childhood that take us right on back to playing in the streets or open fields with kids from the block. Plan a day to teach those games to your kids! Really, DO IT. You'll all have more fun than you know what to do with. If you need some retro-fun-times inspiration, here's another playlist for ya. If you don't know how to make or do some of these, Google them and learn together!

Old-School Shenanigans to Teach Your Kids

---

* Make a comb kazoo.

* Learn to play the spoons and play along to vintage folk music.

* Play jacks.

* Make finger puppets.

* Create shadow puppets when it's dark with a sheet and a flashlight, or on the wall of their bedrooms.

* Learn to blow bubble-gum bubbles (Grape Bubble Yum is the best!).

* Hold a hula hoop contest to your favorite bubblegum pop songs.

* Play Chinese jump rope.

* TAG. Yep, plain old tag. (You'd be mortified at how many kiddos don't know how to play tag. Really, it's mortifying.)

* Play one of these vintage games!

  * Four Square
  * Simon Says
  * Red Light/Green Light
  * Mother, May I
  * Red Rover
  * Pickup Sticks
  * Dominos
  * Marbles
  * Musical Chairs
  * Capture the Flag

LEGO CHALLENGE, KIDS VS. PARENTS

The point of the game is to complete a challenge card with a specific task (e.g.: use only small LEGO blocks, or construct something you'd find on a farm.) Kids and parents, working alone or as a team, can race or compare finished creations at the end of a time period.

First, brainstorm together to come up with ten or twenty challenge cards. These can be written on slips of paper and folded, then placed in a hat or bowl.

Next, take turns picking out a challenge card and read the challenge aloud. Then ready, set, go—complete the challenge!

Bring Back the Poetry Slam

When I taught poetry in my fourth grade classroom, I ended every unit with a "poetry slam." We lit candles, put on soft beatnik music, and my students would choose favorite poems to read out loud to their class-mates. It was so popular that we started doing it sporadically throughout the rest of the school year. That always stuck with me.

One evening at our cottage in Michigan (where I get the majority of my most playful ideas), I brought out my collection of Shel Silverstein books, plopped them on the coffee table, and just started reading a few of his brilliant soliloquies out loud. After my boys finished looking at me like I had clearly extinguished the light in my own attic, they came around and started asking if they could read some aloud too. I don't often toot my own horn, but for more than an hour we all giggled and guffawed and played with the words of this literary genius. Win, win, and win.

Make Board Games Way Less Boring

Board games are quickly becoming a thing of the past. Sad, but oh so true. I work with a lot of toy and game companies, and it always seems harder for their PR folk to get media hits and attention for their board game lines. There's a new video, app, and digital gaming generation in town that would much rather swipe than spin or shuffle. But play-ing traditional board games together teaches kids (and sometimes their parents) interpersonal, social, academic, and emotional skills that can't always be found with controllers alone. So how do we get 'em back to the board? In five simple steps. I've done the research, so you don't have to.

5 Steps to Making Board Games as Appealing as Xbox

1. **SET THE SCENE:** In our new-millennium world of digi everything, old-school board games are often shoved onto a shelf or packed away in a cupboard and rarely retrieved. One way to make them a bit more novel and alluring is to bring them out on a rotating basis, sort of like special guests on your own personal late show. Plop a few out onto the coffee table or on a special card table and begin messing around with them all by yourself, with no encouraging or prodding your kids to join in. It's even better if you act like you really would rather not be bothered or share what you're doing. It makes them want it more. (Humans always want what they think they can't have, no?) Some call this manipulative. I call it genius.

2. **MIX 'EM UP:** Another fun way to bring board games back from the dead is to give your kids three different games, dump out all the pieces, mixing them all up (I know, this makes some of you hyperventilate, but trust me, it'll all be okay), and then ask your kids to invent a whole new game by mixing and mashing pieces and boards for all three. It's crazy the new games they'll invent. And then, when they're all done with the mash-up, help your inventors re-sort and put everything back in its proper box. See, deeeeep breaths; all is well organized once again.

3. **HAVE THEM TEACH YOU HOW TO PLAY:** This one is simple. Act like you are a dingbat and are in great need of help

figuring out a new game. Look befuddled and beg them to help a mama or papa out and show you how it's done. Kids LOVE being smarter than their parents. Let them really believe it once in a while.

....

4. MAKE IT AN EVENT: I did this one night when I really wanted to play Clue and no one would join me in the library with the candlestick. I turned off all the lights, put on spookyish-sounding music, lit candles all around the table, and made some "we haven't got a clue" mystery snacks. They flocked like little Mrs. Peacocks to be a part of the scene. And they still talk about it years later.

....

5. SWAP WITH YOUR FRIENDS: Start a board game group and invite your kids' pals over to share their favorite board games. At the end of the gaming session, put the games that each kid is "bored" with in a pile, and borrow one another's for a few weeks. One person's trash is another person's playful treasure.

Plan a Playground Crawl

Map out three playgrounds in your area that you've never explored, pack a snack picnic, and take your band of players on tour. After you've completed your progressive playdate, return home and vote for "best swings," "most awesome slides," "craziest monkey bars," "lamest playground," etc. A day devoted to playground exploration is kid nirvana.

Celebrate Some of Those Wacky Days of the Year

I simply LOVE those quirky national days of the year like "National Pancake Day," "Blame Someone Else Day," or "Plush Animal Lovers Day." And I think they deserve to be celebrated! Not ALL of them, but the ones that really zing your fun meter. I'm never having a "Vulture Awareness Day" bash (September 5, in case you're into that kind of thing).

Check out daysoftheyear.com for loads of weird and wonderful days of the year to turn into a party.

Paint ... with a Side of Ridiculousness!

Having spent time as a preschool teacher, I know the magnetic nature of a blank canvas, fresh paint, and clean brushes. That trio is hard to resist no matter what your age. I love the idea of keeping a painting easel set up in the kitchen for a few weeks at a time, and quietly switching up the types of tools and kinds of paints available for anyone to explore . . . even YOU. One fun way to play-bomb your kids is to introduce some nontraditional painting tools onto the scene and see what goes down. Give your kiddos large pieces of white construction or finger-painting paper, an easel, covered surface or an "I don't care what happens to this table" table, and then hand over a few of these tools with which to create.

Odd and Wonderful Things to Stick into Paint

* Marbles: Place paper into a shallow cookie pan. Spoon a few blobs of paint onto your paper, and then throw a couple of marbles down into the paint. Holding the sides of the pan, roll the marbles back and forth and around the paint.

* Toothbrushes: Dip, dab, and brush the paint onto your paper using various types and sizes of toothbrushes. It's just fun.

* LEGOs: Stack three or four LEGO bricks of different sizes on top of each other, dip the bumpy tops into paint, and LEGO-print away!

* Apples: Cut several different varieties of apples in half to reveal the "star" in the center. Pour paint into disposable pie tins. Dip the inside of the apple halves into the paint, and use them as stamps. ALWAYS a hit.

* Ice cubes: Squeeze a few drops of food coloring into plastic ice trays. Fill them up with water, cover with plastic wrap, and place a toothpick into each cube. Freeze, pop out, and use the toothpick as your "handle" as you glide the frozen

color across your paper. This one's fun to do outside on a summer day ... see what y'all can paint before your color cubes melt!

* Drinking straws: Put a few dollops of paint onto a piece of white paper that has been set on a cookie sheet or plastic tray. Using plastic drinking straws, have your kids blow the paint around the paper.

* Cars and trucks and things that go: Both boys and girls love to make tracks down and around and all over paper with wheels of any kind. Dip the bottoms of toy cars and trucks into small amounts of paint and zoom them across long sheets of butcher paper you've laid on the floor or taped to a backyard fence, bathtub wall, or other nonprecious surface. Try this with your kids' plastic prehistoric creatures, action figures, and anything else with an unusual "footprint."

* Now that you're open to it, you'll probably begin to recognize all sorts of stuff that would be brilliant to shove into paint. As long as it won't do permanent damage to something ... shove it in!

Okay ... I can hear some of you neat freaks breathing into paper bags. Just use washable kid-paint, and cover your surface with newspaper or a cheap plastic tablecloth (stock up on several of these at the dollar store ... even if they're more than a dollar, they're priceless when it comes to beautiful kid-mess). 'Cause, news flash ... kids freakin' LOVE messing around with paint, and paint is supposed to be messy! That's what makes it so much fun! And it's also why God created paper towels, wet wipes, and bathtubs.

HOMEMADE BATH CRAYONS

What You'll Need

* 1 package of glycerin soap from the craft store
* Glass bowls
* Microwave
* Food coloring
* Ice cube trays

Directions

1. Melt the package of glycerin soap in a glass bowl in the microwave, following the manufacturer's instructions.

2. Divide the melted soap among three or four separate bowls, depending on how many colors you want to create.

3. Add a different color of food coloring to each bowl and stir.

4. Pour the various colors into ice cube trays to harden.

5. Let cool for 1 hour on the countertop.

6. Pop out your bath crayons, draw the kids a bubble bath, and color away!

Camp Out, Inside

Need a dose of crazy playfulness when it's too cold, too hot, or too rainy to romp around outside? Pitch a small tent or teepee in your living room, throw in loads of blankets, pillows, and flashlights, add a batch of stuffed buddies, a basket of favorite books, and a few fun snacks, and let the imaginative bliss begin! This is also an awesome go-to activity on those rough days AFTER your kid has been home sick . . . you know, when they aren't well enough to go to school but are well enough to be bored as bricks at home.

Steal a Preschool Teacher's Secret Weapon: The "Sensory Table"

We called it the "water table" or sensory table back in my preschool teacher days, and it remains every early childhood teacher's secret weapon. You can buy a water/sensory table from classroom supply stores, but they're rather expensive.

If you don't have a couple hundred bucks to drop on a glorified bathtub full of rice or beans and want to whip one up like, today, that's totally doable too.

Start with a large plastic storage bin from a home store (I like the under-the-bed ones). Make sure you get one that is more long and shallow rather than short and deep. Buy the lid too, because you'll want to cover this thing up once the kids are done playing. Unless you've always dreamed of a "sensory carpet."

Spread out a plastic tablecloth (recycle the one from the paint-apalooza I described on page 102) onto an uncarpeted floor. Kitchens work best. If your kitchen is carpeted, then please put this book down immediately and go call a decorator. Go.

Now simply fill up that bin about halfway with the sensory-stimulating stuff of your choice, some kitchen utensils, and any other playful riffraff you think is cool.

This activity is best for kiddos who are down with not sticking every single thing in their pie holes and who understand that the stuff inside sort of needs to stay inside as much as humanly possible. You know your peeps; help them out as needed. Now play, play, play, play, play!

Sensory tubs take full advantage of the element of surprise because you can easily swap out the contents, leaving kids super curious about what they'll find inside next. It's like Christmas morning every time this ever-changing bin of awesome comes out to play.

Here are some of my favorite things to dump into a sensory table or tub:

* Rice: plain or colored with food coloring, short, long, wild, or brown
* Beans of any kind
* Sand
* Water—add food coloring for extra fun
* Snow
* "Clean" soil
* Small uncooked pasta shapes
* Cornmeal
* Oatmeal
* Birdseed
* Hay
* Cereal
* Ice cubes
* Flour
* Popcorn—popped or unpopped
* Shaving cream
* Beads and string

* Glitter. (Please tell me you laid down that cheap plastic tablecloth I told you to buy from the dollar store. Glitter is both heaven and hell, remember?)
* Bubble solution and various wands
* Finger paint
* Buttons
* Shredded paper
* Fall leaves
* Anything you think up that's safe and fun!

Encourage the little hands in your house to scoop, pour, pile, sort, sift, touch, and play with what's inside, however they see fit. Throw in some accessories like funnels, scoops, plastic animals or people, etc., as well. You'll find these sensory tubs are like jelly-covered fingers to a clean white wall. Magnetic. Irresistible.

GLITTERY FLUBBER

What You'll Need

* 2 bottles of white school glue
* ½ cup room-temperature water
* 2 bowls
* GLITTER!
* ½ cup liquid starch

Directions

1. Mix the glue and water together in a separate bowl.

2. Once the mixture is well blended and smooth, add a tablespoon of glitter at a time, mixing it in after each addition.

3. Next, add your glitter mixture to the liquid starch in a separate bowl.

4. Mix and stir . . . your hands work great for this step!

5. PLAY!

Tip: I recommend playing with this fun, gooey substance on a clean table, away from carpeting. If stored covered in the refrigerator, it's good to go for at least a week.

A Harmonica, a Ukulele, and a
Nice Set of Bongos

I love the idea of investing in a few easy-to-play instruments and keeping them within reach, even when no one in your family is particularly musical. We have all three of these easy-to-play song makers around our house, and they are picked up and fiddled with often.

I bought my husband a harmonica for his birthday recently to keep at our unplugged, no-TV, no-Internet lake cottage in hopes he'd learn some campfire songs and go all cowboy on us. Cowboys are hot.

Turns out we all love picking that thing up and getting lost in its breathy notes. We also have a guitar, some bongos, and a ukulele that we encourage houseguests to pick up and play as well. We've had some mighty fun jam sessions spring up out of nowhere, simply because the instruments were there (and the TV wasn't).

Watching kids and grown-ups gather around a living room, smiling and playing out of tune, is all things fabulous. Pretend instruments are fine and dandy when your kiddos are little and still using them as part-time baseball bats. But once they reach age four or five, expose your kids to the real deal and teach them how to play respectfully. You can find lightly used instruments on eBay and at local music shops as well. Go make some joyful and ridiculous noise!

Never, Ever Stop Reading Out Loud … with Silly Voices

Raise your hand if you have read *Goodnight Moon, Curious George Rides a Bike,* or another of your kid's favorite books 567 times . . . just today. Now keep your hand up and give yourself a high five!

Reading great literature out loud to our kids is what we do; it's part of the parental contract. And isn't it lovely how time stands still when we give ourselves over to the glory of a good story? Even when we're weary and sooooo ready for bed, reading out loud is a salve for the busy soul. But as kids get bigger and begin to read on their own, we often say farewell to this playful experience with them. Guess what? Once your kids can read a chapter book on their own, they still long to hear you read to them. For far more years than you may think, actually. They may pretend that they're over it, but do me a favor. Grab one of the books on the next page, curl up in your bed or on the couch with your tween or teen, and just start reading. Out loud. Eventually, they'll get hooked by the story and move a little closer. It might not happen right away, but it will happen. I promise. There is a special force that draws kids and grown-ups together when sharing a good piece of writing. Even after they're too big to sit on your lap.

Well Played

Some of My Favorite "Read-Alouds" for Older Listeners

* *The Search for Delicious*
* *Little Women*
* *Little Men*
* *The Last of the Really Great Whangdoodles*
* *Tuck Everlasting*
* *The Time Machine*
* *The War of the Worlds*
* *Wuthering Heights*
* *To Kill a Mockingbird*
* The Little House series (we read *The Long Winter* every winter)
* *The Indian in the Cupboard* and sequels
* *Peter and the Starcatchers*
* *My Side of the Mountain* ... SUPER FAVORITE!
* The Harry Potter series
* *The Prince and the Pauper*
* *The Hobbit*
* *From the Mixed-up Files of Mrs. Basil E. Frankweiler*

Prepare for Battle

Sometimes conflict is a really good thing. Whether it's a battle fought with big fluffy pillows, water shooters, foam swords, water balloons, or soft yarn balls, don't be afraid to check your ego at the door and jump into a show-down of silly now and again. If you're against anything that blasts, I totally respect that. If you are okay with benign stuff that shoots, then buy thyself some Nerf Blasters pronto (we have an obscene amount of foam dart artillery; please don't ban this book, m-kay?), and BRING IT ON!

Of course there should be "safe play" rules, because this kind of play is not at all about anyone getting hurt. But going gonzo in the basement or backyard with your kids and their nonthreatening weapons of choice will make their day . . . maybe year. And I money-back-guarantee you that letting your inner Katniss Everdeen out for a little romp on the wild side will set your own playful spirit on fire too. For another great resource on "roughhouse" play, you should read *The Art of Roughhousing* by Anthony DeBenedet. It'll make you want to wrestle something.

Puppets Could Pretty Much Rule the World If They Wanted To

We've talked a lot about magical playthings. In my years in the class-room and at home with my boys, what I know for sure is that puppets are at the top of the list of freakishly magical things followed by socks with toes, fake eyelashes, and Strawberry Quik. Ever notice how kids will do almost anything you ask of them when you ask through the hand-driven mouth of a puppet? Use your best Elmo voice for the next sentence: "Elmo says let's go tidy up your room now, Janie!" And your kid just does it, happily, no tantrum, backtalk, or bribe required. FREAKISHLY MAGICAL, I tell you!

After I got my master's degree in education, I had the extreme privilege of working as an educational consultant for a PBS station that shared space with Family Communications, Inc., home of *Mister Rogers' Neighborhood*. I was in my early twenties, and my other young colleagues and I used to sneak down on our lunch breaks and watch Fred Rogers and his amazing team tape episodes of the show. (I may have a picture of me popping out of Mr. Rogers' sweater closet, just saying.) Fred Rogers built a whole neighborhood of make-believe based on the magical and influential powers that puppets possess. Even in my twenties, I would have done pretty much anything King Friday or Queen Sara asked of me.

Puppets have the ability to open kids' imaginations, encourage creative and deeper communication, and invite playful interaction like almost nothing else. A basket full of puppets, a fertile imagination, and a store-bought or homemade puppet theater is the stairway to play heaven.

Find an Old Typewriter and Start Yourself a Story!

One of our most favorite playful activities when we have a big group gathering is "typewriter tales." It all started when my husband found and bought an old typewriter and typing paper on eBay.

Disclaimer: I took a typewriter to college and PAINFULLY wrote and edited papers on that thing for two years, after which I swore I'd never look at another one again. However, a couple of decades later, it turns out typewriters are now vintage, and "hipster," and cool, so here we are.

We all love banging away on the keys and listening to it firmly tap out our words. So back to "typewriter tales." Here's how this creatively fun writing game goes down:

How to Play

1. Feed a piece of typewriter paper into the machine.
2. The story "starter" makes up the first line of a tale, and types it on the top on the page. They can write anything they want (G-rated), but only one sentence.
3. Each person in your group visits the typewriter at any time throughout the party or day, adding only ONE line to the existing story at a time.
4. Guests can read the story before adding their line, but they can add only one complete sentence.
5. Guests can visit and add lines as many times as they like until the designated time is up.
6. At the end of your party or family gathering, read aloud your tale.
7. LOL for reals.

We have done this at several of our family gatherings during the holidays, or during summer reunions and celebrations. And every single time it's downright Hi-larious. It's also a kick to try and guess who wrote which lines. The stories that have been banged out key by key have become treasured reminders of a happy and playful time together.

While there is something unmatched in a vintage typewriter's tappity-tap-tap goodness, even if you don't have one you can still sit with the cool kids. A laptop, iPad, or even a piece of paper and a pencil works just fine too! Kids don't put pencil to paper as much these days with all the keyboarding going on, so this is always a fun and oddly novel alternative.

Puppet-Making Magic

Thankfully, making playful puppets requires very little skill. Jim Henson you need not be. You're making puppets—they're allowed to look silly and a little weird. It's all good. Remember . . . process over product. You don't make fun of your kids' artsy creations, they won't make fun of yours. Usually. Here are three doable ways to make puppets with your kids:

* Wooden spoons: Throw some googly eyes on the back of the oval spoon "head"; glue on some yarn, raffia, or that crinkly paper used to stuff packages on the top as hair; and then dress the handle-body with scraps of fabric.

* Two words . . . lunch bags! I know it's old school, but paper-bag puppets are so darn easy, you won't think twice about making a whole batch and putting on a puppet play. Grab the misfits from your arts and crafts cupboard (you have one of those now, right?), and make 'em as gooney as possible. Easy peasy.

* An old knit glove, a pair of scissors, and those misfits from your craft cupboard again. Simply cut the fingers off an old knit glove, and you have instant finger puppets! Use little googly eyes, felt scraps, yarn, buttons, rickrack, etc. to create a fingertip town of animals and people. You can also use bath gloves, and hot-glue on accents using craft foam, to make waterproof puppets for the tub.

Play-Maker 5 WAYS TO MASTER FAMILY PLAYTIME

Anthony DeBenedet, M.D., coauthor of *The Art of Roughhousing*

1 IT'S PLAY, NOT WORK. Playing with your child or children shouldn't feel like work. But sometimes it can. Ironically, this usually happens when we are thinking about other things that we need to do—like actual work—while we are trying to play. It may sound silly, but the best way to ensure that your family playtime doesn't feel like work is to deliberately set aside time in your schedule for it. Doing this (along with stowing your cell phone away in another country!) will keep you focused on and connected with your child.

2 FUN IS RELATIVE. Parents, especially of older children, often fall into the trap of believing that if they think something is fun, their child will too. But this isn't always the case. Let your child tell you what he or she thinks is fun, and let him or her drive what the activity or playtime looks like. Then go with the flow, even if you're not having much fun (faking it is okay when it comes to playing with your child!).

3 LEAVE LEARNING TILL LATER. You probably know a parent who is always trying to make an educational lesson out of whatever his or her child is doing (e.g., this parent can't just play blocks; he or she must ask the child to count the blocks as they both stack them together). Family playtime should be all about fun, goofing off, and letting loose—not learning. Of course, if learning is a natural byproduct, that's a bonus. Just try not to make it a priority.

115

4. TIMING IS STILL EVERYTHING. For children of any age, dedicated playtime (or simply time) with an undistracted parent equals love. With one big exception: when it follows on the heels of an argument. Sometimes your child, probably like yourself, will need time alone to work through his or her feelings after a disagreement between you or someone else and him or her. Although play has great healing properties, the timing has to be right before you propose having fun together again. Make sure you are available to talk and listen first, and then let your child signal to you when he or she is ready to ramp up the fun again.

5. PLAYTIME WITHOUT "PLAYTIME." Look for small moments of play with your family that may not involve an actual activity. These small moments will often blossom from playful behaviors that are being exhibited by you or your child, such as using one's imagination, being spontaneous, or exercising humor. Make it a point to cherish and honor these moments when they arise. It's often unscripted playfulness that truly connects us to one another and makes play a lasting feature of our family lore for years to come.

Take It Outside

Backyards are for foolishness. It's your patch of green to let your guard down and cut loose. We didn't always have a backyard; we played in parks and on the Chicago lakefront, and on bike trails, etc. So when we got one of our own, we were in total fenced-in bliss.

Sure, it's great to have an outdoor space that's big enough for a sport court, swimming pool, and eighteen-hole golf course. But if you just have a little patch of land, three of the very best investments we've made with our kids over the years are what we call the "backyard trifecta of fun." Anything appended to these three gems adds extra sprinkles and glitter.

Three backyard playmakers that will fully ignite your playful spirit— and never get old. If you have the space, say a big fat "YES!" to these.

THE SANDBOX: If you have the space for a sandbox, it's really a must-do. Just as with the sensory tub we talked about earlier, young children and their folks can't resist a mountain of

sand. The play possibilities are limitless, and when kids and parents sit together and get their hands dirty, time stands still and connection happens.

A BASIC SWING: Whether it's a tire tied to a tree or a full-on swing set, there is nothing, I mean *nothing* like the freedom of gliding through the air, getting higher and higher with every pump. I am a self-professed swingaholic and find great joy in pumping up to the sky. Our playful spirits do a jiggity-jig with every back and forth we take. Even if we're merely the pushers, we can feel its calming and exhilarating goodness. But try not to simply be the pushers all the time. Hop aboard and swing for yourself! Your own playful spirit so totally deserves it.

THE TRAMPOLINE: Trampolines are the vaccines of the playground. Very polarizing and controversial. Some parents find them utterly dangerous and scary, while others are all "They are the most fantastic thing in the whole dang world!" I happen to now be on team most-fab-thing-ever. This has everything to do with the fact that we have a super-safe Springfree trampoline. My husband did a slew of research on these bounce machines before we bought one, and this one came out as the safest and most durable. I call Springfree tramps the Dyson of trampolines. No joke, this is the one piece of backyard equipment that NEVER gets old, and evokes the most joy. I should also say that a batch of middle-aged moms on that thing is some of the best comedy around.

Okay, so you don't have the time, money, or space for big backyard playthings. I get that. My husband and I lived in a condo in Chicago with no green space of our own until our first son was three years old.

Before migrating to a suburb of Chicago, we logged a lot of hours playing out on the front stoop, down by the lakefront, and over at the city playgrounds. I think in some ways not having our own private space in those early years made us more playful as a family. It took intention and planning, not just letting the kids out into the backyard.

We took outings to find fun spaces out of necessity. And that collective playfulness stuck with us as our next boy came along and we got a patch of green all to ourselves. So much of our willingness to leap into playful experiences with our kids comes down to a simple and purposeful shift in our perspective. Do we think of play as "their" thing, and we gift them with our presence now and again? Or do we think of playfulness as ours too? Please don't think I mean that parents need to play with their kids all the time. Kids need their own playtime just like we do. But it's the notion that it's always available to us, and the fact that they LOVE it when we jump in and "go there"—that's the shift. So go there sometimes—really GO THERE. It'll make you a happier human being.

119

Simple and Surefire Ways to Get Your Family Lost in Outside Play

* **INSTANT OBSTACLE COURSES:** This is a two-for-one family activity. Clean out your garage while creating a wicked cool outdoor course for your kids! Simply grab all of your random sports equipment and backyard toys like jump ropes, hula hoops, little orange cones, play tunnels, various sizes of balls, etc., and have your kids design an obstacle course in the backyard or nearby park. Then invite their friends over for some time trials.

* **AN OUTDOOR SOUND WALL:** aka ... let's clean out the kitchen cupboards! (Check out the Doable DIY on page 122 for directions.)

* **LOADS OF PLAYGROUND BALLS:** We've found housing our large collection of basketballs, whiffle balls, playground balls, footballs, etc., in a collapsible garden bin makes for easy cleanup and storage. Kids love balls. Dump them out as often as possible, and join the game.

* **SIDEWALK CHALK, NEON CHALK, AND GLOW CHALK, OH MY!** Sidewalk chalk is the cockroach of play. It seems to multiply, and once you have some, it seems to never really disappear. Unlike the roach, however, sidewalk chalk is an instant mood booster. We like to draw frames on our front sidewalk,

leave chalk out, and write a note beside it to encourage passersby to draw something in the frames!

* A ZIP LINE: We recently installed a tree-to-tree zip line at our cottage in Michigan, and it was worth every penny and hour of installation. If you have the space, have the grandparents chip in on this family gift. Flying through the air on a wire is good fun.

* POGO STICKS AND KID STILTS: You'll be scared to get on these at first. And then you won't want to get off.

* HULA HOOPS: 'Nuff said.

* PUSH SCOOTERS: . . . for everyone in the family

* A BABY POOL: Fill it with water, or sand, or dirt, or mulch.

* JUMP ROPES BOTH SHORT AND LONG: When's the last time you did a little double Dutch of your own?

CREATING A BACKYARD SOUND WALL

I first saw a "sound wall" at a progressive preschool and was truly in awe at how intoxicating it was for the children. The great news is that it's totally easy to create in your very own backyard. All you need is a length of wooden fence from your local home store and a batch of odds and ends from your kitchen or a thrift store with which to create the instruments. Think old lightweight pots and pans, colanders, Bundt pans, metal pot lids, tin gelatin molds, ice cube trays, old washboards, and on and on and on. Attach each item to the fence with nails or rope. Hand your kiddo a wooden spoon, metal whisk, or other kitchen utensil, and let the "music" begin!

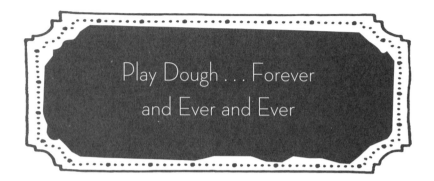

Play Dough . . . Forever
and Ever and Ever

There is a really good reason kids have been playing with dough for like EVER. It feels great in their hands, it can turn into anything they want, it's completely open-ended, and the smashing, and mashing, and rolling, and shaping involved is totally therapeutic. If you're in a dumpy, grumpy mood, bash a bit of dough with your kids and you'll feel a whole bunch better. I promise. Here are four of my all-time favorite play dough recipes.

BEST BASIC PLAY DOUGH RECIPE

What You'll Need

* 2 cups flour
* 2 cups warm water
* 1 cup salt
* 2 tablespoons vegetable oil
* 1 tablespoon cream of tartar
* Food coloring (you can also use unsweetened drink mix)

Directions

1. Mix all the ingredients together, and stir over low heat. Keep stirring until the mixture begins to resemble mashed potatoes. When the dough pulls away from the sides, remove from heat and let cool. If it's too sticky, just keep stirring and cooking until it feels like Play-Doh.

2. Add your desired colors and let the play begin!

3. If you store this dough in the fridge, it will last for up to a month.

KINETIC SAND

What You'll Need

* 6 cups play sand (available inexpensively at home improvement stores)
* 1 ½ cups cornstarch
* 2 teaspoons dish soap
* ¾ cup water

Directions

1. In a large bin, combine the play sand and cornstarch and mix really well.

   ....

2. Combine the soap and water in a separate container, and stir until the water gets bubbly.

   ....

3. Pour the soapy water into the sand and cornstarch mixture, and mix well. Keep mixing before adding any further water. Add slightly more water until the mixture is the desired consistency.

Tip: If you feel like you need to revive your kinetic sand, simply add a touch more soap. This will give it the fun squishy texture kids love.

THE AMAZING OOBLECK "DOUGH"

This is probably the easiest and most fun play mixture you can make with two ingredients! Whip it up whenever the natives get restless.

What You'll Need

1 cup cornstarch
½ cup water
Food coloring (optional)

Directions

Pour the cornstarch in a large bowl and gently break up any lumps with your fingers. Slowly pour the water into the cornstarch, mixing with a spoon. Add a couple of drops of food coloring, if desired, and mix well.

I like to make big batches of this crazy solution and place it in big bowls on the counter. The cool thing about "oobleck" is that there's a whole bunch of science behind it as well. When your kids move it quickly around in their hands, it becomes a solid. When they stop playing with it, it goes back to being a liquid. This makes for some mighty fun experimenting.

FOAM DOUGH

This is the easiest foam dough to make!

What You'll Need

* Shaving cream
* Cornstarch
* Food coloring
* Measuring cups
* Play dough tools, molds, your imagination

Directions

1. Measure out any amount of cornstarch in a bowl.

2. Spray about the same amount of shaving cream on top!

3. Mix it together with your hands until you get a "moldable" dough.

4. Add small drops of food coloring as you mix.

5. Use your molds and tools to mash, smash, mold, and PLAY.

Tip: You can add a little more cornstarch or shaving cream as you play to create the consistency you're looking for.

Play
with Your

"Playfulness in a relationship is like the fizz in champagne"

\- ANONYMOUS

Mate

I met my six-foot-seven high school sweetheart when I was fifteen. We dated, we fell in love, and then I married him two weeks after my twenty-first birthday, having just graduated from college in three years, because I promised my parents I'd graduate first and was so in love I JUST COULDN'T WAIT. Three cheers for young, crazy love!

Please know that I'm really not a proponent of getting married super young as a rule, but it worked for us, and we've had a blast growing up together. We like each other a lot. We're one of those duos who would honestly really rather be with each other than anyone else, and equally important, we still get each other's motors revving.

Our kids think it's slightly nauseating.

If you are in mid-gag right now over how Disney movie my marriage sounds, make no mistake. Our longevity and deep liking of each other after all this time is not due to dumb luck, kismet, moon alignment, or seven dwarves and a magic kiss. We work hard at our playful relationship. Not like ditchdigging kind of hard, more like learning to do a backflip on a trampoline kind of hard. The practice and learning and working at it are still really enjoyable work. Bouncing always trumps digging.

Jon and I are about to celebrate twenty-five years of legally hanging out together, and looking back, a whole lot of "stuff" has happened in my life between the ages of twenty-one and fortysomething. Stuff like jobs and moves, houses and babies, toddlers who turn into teenagers and then leave for college, more moves, sickness, health, better, worse, ups, downs, and all sorts of in-betweens.

Any time two humans decide to cohabitate and raise other humans, there's going to be a marked learning curve and some bumps in the road.

I'm an instant over-reactor; my husband is a slooooow burn. I see DEFCON 4, and he sees a skinned knee. I'm a "guts and go!" kinda gal. He's a "let me ponder that for a quick millennium" kinda man. He approaches "issues" with goofy humor and a "there are really very few catastrophes" filter, and I am finally learning to take his slightly maddening advice to "pump my brakes," take a cleansing breath or a hot bath, and put "catastrophes" into perspective.

Most days.

And while shared faith, unshakable love, respect, and understanding are certainly the cornerstones of a really awesome long haul, without a doubt if you aren't creating and having some serious fun, and playing together as much as possible along the way, that haul is a whole lot heavier. Sometimes that haul will even be seemingly impossible.

I'm not standing on a glitter-covered soapbox preaching that a playful spirit is the MOST vital ingredient in the complex stew that is a still-in-love-after-a-million-years relationship. If it were, only grumpy, boring, serious people would get divorced. Marriage takes a batch of quality ingredients to stay fresh and delicious long after the date of purchase.

But after being hitched to the same guy for a quarter century, what I know for absolutely sure is this: Our willingness to let our grown-up facades fall away now and again and playfully experience this crazy, complicated life unleashes an uninhibited bonding joy and trusting vulnerability that becomes a salty-sweet seasoning that helps keep a relationship yummy and well preserved.

What Would Maria Do?

Relationships, especially married-with-kid ones, require a whole mess of dirty work. It's often a caffeine-injected daily grind filled to the brim with serious, not-at-all-playful responsibilities requiring us to be full-on grown-ups much of the time. And that magically delicious mash-up of working, parenting, mortgages, parent-teacher conferences, picky eaters, lost luggage, supervising homework (I mean, homework *alone*, am I right?) can be kind of overwhelming and fun-crushing to the folks in charge. Honestly, aren't you still sort of shocked that we've been put in charge of these little human beings? Most of us are making it up as we go, and holding on for dear life. Let's get real . . . no one really knows WTF they're doing, and "parenting expert" is the biggest oxymoron that ever lived.

So how do we purposefully inject more playfulness and frivolity into our relationships with our best mates? Well, in the words of Maria from *The Sound of Music,* "Let's start at the very beginning, a very good place to start."

In *The Sound of Music,* Maria single-handedly made a bundle of play clothes out of overpriced European curtains . . . without a YouTube tutorial, Google, or glass of Chardonnay. The other moms in the subdivision probably hated her, but one thing's for certain: That girl knew how to play. So in moments when I feel like telling my husband "so long, farewell, *auf Wiedersehen,* good-bye," I try to ask myself "What would Maria do?"

The Dating Game

Apart from arranged marriages and crazy reality shows like *Married at First Sight*, in which two people meet for the first time at the altar, all relationships generally begin with some form of dating scenario. You know, that special time where two people awkwardly try and get to know each other in order to determine if they could one day be cool sharing a bathroom, and the rest of their lives together?

Dating is exciting and flirty and fun. It's how we fall in love with someone.

If you're in the throes of falling in love as we speak, make sure you're exploring your potential mate's playful side along with their front side and backside! How someone handles a water balloon to the face is a pretty good indicator of how they'll parent a toddler. You'll send me flowers later for this little insight.

Need a picture of your significant other's play aptitude? Engage in a few of the following playdates.

1. Water balloons, Super Soakers, and sprinklers, oh my. It starts with young fun and ends with wet T-shirts and a hot shower. Everyone's a winner.
2. Go to an amusement park and play some of the rip-off carnival games. If he says "It's not worth the money" . . . run.
3. Do some country line dancing. One must be able to check their ego at the "Okay, No Way," Corral.
4. Saunter through the toy aisle. Next time you're at Target together, take a turn into toy land and ask him which were his favorites as a kid. If he gets all excited standing in front of the Star Wars action figures, he's a keeper. He gets bonus points if he makes Chewbacca noises.
5. Work on a thousand-piece jigsaw puzzle together. If he builds a solid foundation first, then lets you put in the last piece, and you're still dating when you've finished . . . you'll be married for fifty years.
6. Go bowling. Competition, gutters, and big balls. 'Nuff said.
7. Helium-filled balloons and a bottle of bubbly. Suck them both down some night and see who laughs the hardest.
8. Play a serious game of Risk. Three hours into the game, you'll see how much of a dick-tator he can be.
9. A friendly game of anything you're better at than him. Marry a good winner, and a better loser.
10. Check out a celebrity impersonator show. You want to be with someone who will stand up and cheer for a fake Bruce Springsteen. I fell more in love with my now husband when I saw him do this in Myrtle Beach back in the '90s.

GIANT OUTDOOR TIC-TAC-TOE

What You'll Need

* Roll of colorful duct tape
* Shower curtain
* 6 Frisbees: 3 of one color and 3 of another

Directions

1. Use the duct tape to create a tic-tac-toe grid (nine squares) on your shower curtain.

2. Lay the shower curtain on your lawn and choose a point for players to stand behind to toss their Frisbees. You may want to pin down the corners of your shower curtain with a few rocks or other heavy objects.

3. Players take turns tossing their Frisbee onto the shower curtain. This might take some practice, but by the end of summer, your kids will be Frisbee pros!

Now back to marriage and dating. It's totally cliché, but vitally important to keep the courtship alive and well the longer you've been hitched. Women never tire of being courted, and men never tire of the connection that happens on the court.

However, the idea of "courting" or "wooing" the person you love, especially once the rings are on and sex suddenly requires a shot of espresso, fully sleeping children, finding a razor (maybe), and a very sturdy lock on the door, becomes more work than it seems like it's worth. Who has the tiiiiime?

Then add in our new technological landscape of texting, Skyping, Facebook messaging, and emoticon-filled love notes, and we're screwed (and by screwed I mean not actually getting screwed). Make no mistake, I'm a major fan of witty, high-speed flirt-athons via text message or Snapchat, and I'm fairly certain there is a boob shot of me, left over from one of my husband's work trips, still floating around somewhere on the Cloud.

But love and longevity can't survive on text messages alone. If we want our relationship with our partner to stay fresh-ish, exciting, and fun, we need to work at playing.

This past spring, the topic of "promposals" hit the zeitgeist once again. Promposals are a relatively new tradition of asking someone to go to prom in an over-the-top, creative, and often ridiculous way. High school "promposals" might be getting a touch out of hand, but ya know what? I want one! The effort, the romance, and cheesy public displays of affection all wrapped up in goofy teenage love? Sign me up! Imagine how far a promposal-like date invitation from your mate would go in the midst of your married-with-children existence?

Whether it's your first date or your four hundredth, making your dates with your mates more playful and adventurous doesn't just make them more fun, it gives them the superpower of bringing you closer together. Just like with our kids, our partners will usually open up and

reveal more of who they are when they're engaged in a playful experience. To play is to cooperate. Cooperation breeds communication, and communication breeds connection. It's a beautiful ring of fire.

9 Dates That Are Way Better than Dinner and a Movie

1 GET SEMICOMPETITIVE WITH YOUR MATE. Play ANYTHING on separate teams, and play to win.

2 TRIPLET DATING. I'm aware this sounds like the latest reality show on TLC; stick with me here. Gathering two or three of your most favorite couples and planning a playful outing will take you back to high school and group-date giddiness. Find out what fun new thing is happening in your 'hood. Go see a comedian, take a Segway tour around your town, or get tickets to a concert in the park and bring along glow sticks and a light-up Frisbee (those exist). Whatever it is, pour yourselves into that minivan and roll, people!

3 DRIVE TO A NEARBY NEIGHBORHOOD OR TOWN YOU'VE NEVER VISITED, and explore its main street on foot without making any reservations or plans ahead of time. Go where the spontaneous road leads.

4 PLAY IN THE DIRT. Working on an outside project that requires you to get dirty and messy and tangled up together can be

super sexy and connective. Getting your hands in the ground to make something more beautiful is hot. It also requires a shower afterward. Just saying.

5. SURPRISE YOUR MATE with a picnic dinner in a park or by the shore. Other couples will walk by and wish they were as awesome as you are.

6. HIRE A PERSONAL CHEF for just a few hours, and have him or her teach you both how to create a dish from your favorite restaurant. Then set the table for two, kick the chef out of your house, and enjoy your date night IN. Pro tip: Consider hiring a tween or teen in your neighborhood to be a "mother's helper" and play with your kids while you and your mate play in the kitchen.

7. COOK SOMETHING TOGETHER you can't even pronounce. Something French should do the trick.

8. WALK HAND IN HAND through a local museum exhibit. Talk about what you see in the pieces amid the quiet calm of the gallery.

9. CREATE SOMETHING TOGETHER that you have no skill at creating. I'm pretty terrible at shooting hoops, and while my husband can technically carry a tune, neither of these facts keep us from playing a game of one-on-one or kicking up the karaoke now and again.

Play Maker 5 PLAYFUL DATES

Bela Gandhi, creator and CEO of Smart Dating Academy, and dating guru for *The Steve Harvey Show*

I've had several great convos with my friend Bela Gandhi about the role playfulness "plays" in two people falling and staying in love. She has seen it all, let me tell you. So I asked her to share five playful dates that she thinks not only light the fire but keep it burnin'.

1. **PAINT A HUGE CANVAS TOGETHER:** There is nothing like creating together, and it is a BLAST to get some acrylic paints, a big canvas, and a good bottle of wine! You can proudly display your co-creation above the mantel!

2. **TAKE A DANCE CLASS:** Nothing is more fun than getting close, and some awesome tunes (even if you have two left feet). Salsa or merengue can be particularly alluring with the hip swaying, and is a wonderful time (and easy to learn)! Then, you'll impress your pals at the next wedding or fundraiser you attend with your ability to cut a rug! We learned to tango and are taking a ballroom class as we speak!

3. **GET SCARED TOGETHER:** Generating adrenaline is shown to increase attraction! Rent a scary movie, or if it's in season, go to a haunted house. If you're afraid of heights, take an acro yoga class (the kind where you're suspended from the ceiling). Or if you're in Chicago, head over to the Sears Tower where you can step out onto the glass—and look down together.

4. HAVE A *FERRIS BUELLER'S DAY OFF* DATE DAY: This should be in your own city—doing everything that your heart desires, or is the best-of in your city! Start with an excellent breakfast at your favorite spot, take a morning bike ride along the water, have lunch at a fine French restaurant, see a ballgame, go to an art gallery, and end up back at home snuggling by the fireplace.

5. GO ON A PROGRESSIVE DINNER DATE: This is fun whether you're newly dating or have been together for years. Sleuth out your mate's favorite drinks, appetizer, entrée, and dessert spots—and hire a car to go from place to place to enjoy ONLY their favorites!! My husband did this for me—and it was AWESOME! Epic smile emoticon.

BONUS: The Mock Restaurant

This bonus idea is brilliant for slightly older kids and a special occasion. And it made for my most favorite anniversary night ever. When my boys were seven and eleven years old, they creatively re-created one of our favorite restaurants from our dating days. It was an Italian restaurant called Bruno's, and we used to go all the time in high school and college. I gave the boys the idea, and they ate it up.

We picked a menu that was easy enough for them to make almost all by themselves. They created a sign that said "Bruno's 2" that they hung in our dining room, set the table all pretty, and got into dressy clothes to be our waiters. When their dad arrived home, they greeted him at the door, took his coat, and led him to the "restaurant." I got all dressed up too, and we sat at the candlelit table while the boys took our orders (there was one thing on the menu), and served us. They took it very seriously, and it was adorable. I actually wouldn't wait for a special occasion to do this idea. Have your kids serve you as soon as possible. They owe you.

Have I sufficiently convinced you that big servings of playfulness truly does make our romantic relationships more supercalifragilistic?

If not, I'd like you to shut this book immediately, take a nap, and have some Skittles. And then give me a call so we can have a little chat.

If I have, then round of applause! My publisher will be so happy! Now keep on reading, because here are a batch of simple and fun ways you can be more playful with your mate right this very minute.

If you want to add more fun and frivolity to your marriage or partnership, but y'all's courting creativity has up and left the corral, it's time to dust off your lasso and get back in the saddle. What follows is a bushel of ways to play more with your mate. These are meant to inspire and invigorate and become the catalyst for your own creative ideas. If you're

ready to reconnect with that person you fell in love with, or unearth your mate's decomposing playful spirit, as well as your own, then grab your hobby horse and let's ride!

Don't Be Afraid to Look a Fool ... It's Totally Endearing

Once you've been in a committed relationship for a while and have reached the milestone of being totally down with flossing, burping, and peeing in front of each other, fear not! You haven't merely relinquished a large chunk of romantic mystery, you've now entered the sweet spot of familiarity that, while sometimes slightly disgusting, is also wildly freeing.

Congratu-freakin-lations! You can now act like complete morons in front of each other and remain confident your significant other will still be there in the morning!

That's some good stuff right there.

Abduct Your Spouse ...

For lunch, for the night, for a weekend, for a quickie in a by-the-hour hotel room—doesn't matter. It's the ACT of snatching them away that's the golden ticket here. Just make whatever you choose to do lighthearted and playful. Easy. If you make it a surprise, all the better.

We all want to feel whisked away now and again, don't we? I do. And it's not just the guys who should be doing the whisking. Dudes love it too . . . but don't ask them, 'cause they won't admit it. They love it, I tell you. It's 2016, we're all equal here, right? One of my most favorite dates with my man was a "long lunch" date. It lasted a whole hour and a half. I hopped the train into the city of Chicago from our northern suburb, gathered him from his office, and treated him to lunch and a walk through the modern wing of our art institute. We had a midday cocktail (so scandalous!), focused on each other, without interruption, chatted not about the kids, and then walked to the museum and strolled through beautiful works of art pretending to be aficionados. Then I hopped back on the train, he went back to work, and we couldn't wait to see each other again that night. Fore-PLAY at its best.

Opposite Day

When my boys were very young, they once pulled the "opposite day" stunt on an unsuspecting and very sweet teenage babysitter, with catastrophic results. She apparently wasn't made aware that it was opposite day in their personal land of make-believe and therefore clueless to the fact that all of her commands and requests would be promptly granted . . . only with the opposite of what she asked. Terrible little children. (Sorry again, Amanda!)

While evil in the hands of small children, within a grown-up relationship "Opposite Day" can be miraculous. While safety and familiarity creates fertile ground for playfulness in a relationship, an overdose of predictability and routine can swallow the fun in a long-term union right up. Like, eat it ALIVE.

Love should never be more mundane than magic and sometimes we need to do the polar opposite of what our mate expects us to do. Because surprise equals winning! And playful equals good. Just make sure to use your opposite-day powers for good, unlike my little juvenile delinquents. They've turned out to be very nice young men, BTW.

Keep Those Card Companies in Business

When was the last time you received a hold-in-your-hand card from your significant other, when it wasn't your birthday or anniversary or some other required card-sending holiday? Real cards are cheap and sweet and fun! Let's send more of them! Especially to that person you sleep next to every night. Stock up when you're at the grocery or drugstore, and whip one out when your mate least expects it but needs it the most. Every February 15, I go and grab a batch of fifty-percent-off sappy Valentine's Day cards and stash them away in my bedside table. When I'm feeling frisky or disconnected from my guy, I sneak one under his pillow, onto his windshield, or inside his luggage before a work trip.

How to Use Opposite Day for Good

It won't suck, I promise. If you don't think you need to put Opposite Day on your calendar, but nod like a bobblehead while reading any of the following statements, it's time to mix things up and infuse some creative playfulness into your love-nest.

Opposite Day is merely doing the opposite of what you ALWAYS do. Trust me, just swerve slightly out of your safety lane for twenty-four hours and see what happens.

* You ALWAYS wear full-coverage underthings, because the notion of a thong makes you dry heave. (Cosabella makes miraculous thongs and other sexy unmentionables that will change your life. And not make you hurl.)

* 1-800-FLOWERS is programmed into your cell, they have your credit card on file, and they know you by name.

* Dinner and a movie, dinner and a movie, dinner and a movie. Also known as the *Groundhog Day* of dating.

* Your sexiest jammies have a college name written across the chest, a drawstring, or built-in socks.

* Sex only on the weekends. If he's lucky and you aren't bloated.

* Sex only in your bed. Only. On the weekends, and if you aren't bloated.

* Netflix, Netflix, Netflix, Netflix, Netflix. Every single mother-loving night.

Buy Yourself Some Toys!

(The ones you'd be mortified if your kids found in the back of your closet. You can blush all you want, but a blindfold and some body paint make a Tuesday night way more interesting.)

Steal Your Children's Toys

Raise your hand if you've ever bought your kids a toy, game, or other plaything because you really just thought it would be big fun to play with it all by yourself? If you haven't, what the Nerf Blaster are you waiting for?! One of the benefits of having these needy little creatures in our houses is that we have the opportunity to relive a bit of our own childhoods. So get on that, will ya?

I'm not talking about living vicariously though your children or helicoptering over them at the playground, so save your precious 140 characters.

I am, however, suggesting using your little players as pawns in your own pursuit of a really good time. Why not take advantage of the play pimps you have living in your house and eating all your food? You made them. The least they can do is share their Super Soakers, kick scooters, trampolines, and Xbox. Playing full-on with your kids can be enlivening if you stop looking at it as a guilt-induced chore that's all for their benefit. It's fun to play altogether. But just as your kids need time to play alone, and with their best buds, so do y'all. Scan the playroom, steal their stuff, wait till they aren't around, and let the games begin!

10 Ways to Transform Your Children's Toys into Ridiculous Playtime with Your Partner

1. Be utterly moronic on a trampoline with your husband for fifteen minutes before bedtime.

2. Spray each other down with Super Soakers on a summer night after the kids go to bed. A white tank top on your part would send this over the top. It's your husband, so it's not sexist—make him wear one too if that helps.

3. Fire up the video game system and go head-to-head in Mario Kart or Disney Infinity. FYI: Merida is fierce. Be her.

4. Play "vino pong"—it's beer pong's classier cousin with a master's degree and a Montblanc pen. (If you don't have a Ping-Pong table, buy a set that converts your dining room table.)

5. Two words: pillow fight.

6. That basketball hoop you bought for the backyard? Go one-on-one with each other, playing horse or pig or "Minivan."

No hoop? No problem. Every elementary school playground in your neighborhood has one. Wait till after hours, bring a boom box with your favorite tunes, and shoot around a little at dusk. How adorable will you two be?

7. Become swingers. On your backyard swing set. Make sure to install one or two swings strong enough to hold a couple of grown ups.

8. Strip Scrabble. Every three words you win, your partner has to remove something. I recommend lots of layers, closed blinds, and cheating.

9. Any preschool board game can be quite easily turned into a drinking game. Think about it for thirty seconds, and it'll become clear. Most of them look like they were developed while partially inebriated . . . Candy Land? Chutes and Ladders? Come on.

10. Nerf Blasters, foam darts, your bedroom, nine P.M. Be there. Locked and loaded.

LAWN SCRABBLE

What You'll Need

* About 9 (1 x 6) wooden boards
* 4 short stakes
* Nylon rope
* White paint
* Black paint
* Paper
* Utility knife
* Power drill and drill bits
* Tape measure
* Saw
* Sandpaper

Directions

1. Sand the surface of the boards and paint them white. Allow to dry.

2. Measure and mark 6 inches from the end of the board and cut. Use this square to mark along the board, then cut. Repeat with all the boards until you have 100 squares.

3. Print 4 x 4-inch letters of the alphabet on separate sheets of paper, then cut out the letters to make stencils.

4. Position stencil on top of each dry tile and paint black. Make these amounts: E (10); A (8); R, I, O, T, N (7); S, L, C (5); D, U (4); P, M, H (3); G, B, F, Y (2); J, W, K, V, X, Z, Q (1).

5. Measure and mark 2 inches down from top of short stakes and drill a hole large enough for the nylon cord. Repeat with the remaining stakes.

6. Thread the nylon rope between two short stakes and knot it. Repeat to make a second tile holder.

7. Drive the stakes into the ground, making sure the rope is taut and the tile holders face away from each other. Put the tiles facedown on the ground. Each player selects 7 tiles and places them along their rope holder. Let the word games begin!

Secret Date Night

I came up with this next idea as a way of using my manipulative powers for good. See, there are some things I have always wanted to try with my husband that I knew he'd never agree to. Ballroom dancing was at the top of that list. I knew we'd have a "ball" if I could just get his size-fifteen feet in the building. Thus "secret date night" was hatched. I planned for a beginner dance lesson and told him what time to be ready and what to wear. The rest was a secret. Not gonna lie, he nearly fled the scene when we pulled up to the dance studio, his only words being "no you didn't." But an hour of imperfect pasodobles, cheesy cha-cha-chas, incessant giggling, and feeling like we were back at the junior prom? Priceless. We've spent the last year taking turns surprising each other with one goofball date after another. Sometimes secrets between a husband and wife are a very good thing.

Let Him See You Sweat

My husband and I generally work out separately. Taking turns, like most couples with kids, we alternate manning the fort at home while the other gets ripped. But once our boys were old enough to be alone for an hour in the early morning, we decided to hit the gym together before they woke up. If you have never worked out with your partner, you need to know that it's surprisingly sexy and can be one of the best aphrodisiacs on the market. Watching each other move and sweat and pretend to still be athletic-ish is just fun and will remind you what a stud your partner is. Playing in the gym or outdoors and getting fit also creates a sense of being a part of the same team. You encourage each other to try new things and break through barriers.

8 Playful Ways to Get Sweaty and Fit Together

1. Go for a run, and in the homestretch, race each other. (The boy doesn't always win, just FYI.)

2. Grab the playground equipment. Hula hoop, jump rope, play tag.

3. Take weekly power hikes, suburban strolls, or city-block walks. Skip down at least one street or path along the way. Seriously. You'll look ridiculous, and it will make your day.

4. Downward dogs, warrior pose, and sun salutations, oh my. Yoga can be super sexy. All that bending and stretching and heavy breathing? Boom.

5. Have longer sex. About two hundred calories burned per healthy session, according to some studies! That's a donut, girls. Let's do this.

6. Sign up for semiprivate swim lessons together and learn more than just the breast and backstroke.

7. Register for a fun 5K like a warrior run, color run, bubble run, etc., and be each other's training buddies.

8. Create a simple playground circuit training course at your local park, making the monkey bars, seesaw, and park

benches your gym, and those kids of yours, your personal trainers.

Do Something Altogether Foolish or Moderately Risky

In my chat with Bela Gandhi, she told me that when we get excited or scared along with someone, our body pumps up the adrenaline, and adrenaline creates attraction. She sees it all the time in her matchmaking business, and it's why she encourages her newly dating couples to take risks and be playful with one another. She explained that it's not the fear-for- your-life kind of fear but that nervous, slightly apprehensive type of energy that makes one's heart beat a little faster and that draws folks together. "When you're in an exciting, suspenseful, or slightly scary situation, your desire to have someone to hold on to or pull you close kicks in." Makes total sense, right?

Here's how to get us some of that:

* Skinny-dip together. If you have access to a lake, an ocean, or a private pool, you have to do this at least once . . . a year. Nothing beats the daring, flirty freedom of baring it all. One shot of tequila and I'm always the first one in. Just know where you've left your gutchies.
* Hit an amusement park for your next date, and ride all the roller coasters. Don't tell your kids you went without them. They'll hate you.
* Go to a drive-in movie and see something a little frightening. Making out in the backseat makes fear instantly go away.
* Plan an overnight backpacking or camping trip and protect each other from the bears.

* Act like an adrenaline junkie for a day. Go zip lining, go-kart racing, or bungee jumping together. The "love hormone" oxytocin is also triggered by a touch of fear, so start your engines, people!

* Find a circus arts class in your area, and try the trapeze together. Remember, no posting pics of any of this on social media, so you can look as awkward as you want!

* Perform together: Play in a band, try out for a play, or go to open-mic night and tell stories or jokes. Even if you're not good at all. Especially if you're not good at all.

* Join a couples volleyball, softball, bowling, or paddle tennis team together. Playing for the same team feels adorable and very seventeen-year-old.

* Take a painting, drawing, writing, or sculpting class together. Learning something new creates vulnerability in both of you. And showing vulnerability breeds trust, compassion, and attraction.

* Explore the slightly risky adventures available in your own city, town, or neighborhood and get a few on the calendar. White-water rafting, helicopter rides, fly fishing, horseback riding—whatever it is in your neck of the woods that screams "I dare you," do it together.

Run Away from Home and Explore Your Own City or Town like a Tourist

No matter where you call home, there are things in your city or neighborhood you take for granted or think are for "the tourists." I grew up in a little town in western Pennsylvania called Indiana. I know, that's the name of a state too. I get it.

Indiana's surrounding villages have names like "Black Lick," "Creekside," and "Cherry Tree." You get the picture. But just about an hour away from our sleepy university town is the city of Pittsburgh. It was the place we'd run off to for adventure when we were in college. Pittsburgh is a city of diverse and super fun neighborhoods, all with their own quirky personalities. Jon and I lived in Pittsburgh for a couple of years before we had kids and good paying jobs. With not much money for elaborate date nights, we often went neighborhood hopping, in search of cheap thrills. Now that we live in Chicago, and actually have money to spend on big fancy dates, we still really enjoy being all touristy in our own town. Chinatown for dinner, "staycation" overnights in one of the beautiful downtown hotels, boat tours on the Chicago River, checking out a museum exhibit, or catching a show at Second City. Sometimes it's fun to pretend you're from out of town and pick one of the most touristy or cheesy things to do in your own hometown.

Make a list here of the top five things your town or city's tourist bureau or Chamber of Commerce recommends as a "must-do" for visitors.

1. _____
2. _____
3. _____
4. _____
5. _____

How many of these have you and your partner done? Pick a few and slap them on your calendar for an upcoming date. If you've done 'em all . . . high five! Now go find five more.

Go Old School

Re-Create the Way You Were

My husband and I started dating in 1985. We were teenagers and dated like teenagers do. Innocent and old school. But whether you met your mate in high school, college, or last year, there is something fun and flirty about taking a make-believe trip back in time and dating like they did "back in the day." No DeLorean necessary.

* Put the needle on the record. Vinyl is back with a vengeance. Dust off your old record player, or buy a brand-new one and spin.
* Search for an old-school drive-in movie theater in your area, or re-create one in your driveway with a projector system and a white bedsheet attached to the garage door. Milk Duds, anyone?

* Mini golf, milk shakes, and a make-out session at a lookout point. Party like it's 1959.
* Go see a rock band you know nothing about. Remember being in high school or college and going to see LIVE music at cheap dive bars? Yeah, let's see you do that again. Even if you have to leave after the first set because it's too loud and you can't see the drink menu without your readers.
* Sneak into a public swimming pool, down to the beach, or into a park after hours. I used to do this with my crazy friends in high school, over at Mack Park community pool, and there is some kind of sexy fun in bending the rules just a bit. I always kept my clothes on, for the record.

Bust Out the PDA

Make room for too-long hugs, holding hands while you walk, and flirting interactions in public, like you did when you were teenager. Why do we ever stop making OUT with our mates? From the time my boys were toddlers they would routinely wriggle in between their dad and me at the first glimpse of canoodling of any kind, nudging us apart with their little elbows and hips. My son Truman is now thirteen and still gives us a "Whoa, whoa, whoa, back that train up!" when we sneak a little somethin'-somethin' in the kitchen or while out walking the dog. I always tell him it's better than his dad and me NOT wanting to hold each other's hands or give each other smooches because we don't like each other anymore. That usually quells the disgust a touch.

Here are some ways to throw in a dollop of playful PDA the next time you and your legally bound boyfriend are out and about together:

Well Played

1. GRAB HIS HAND! The next time you're walking along together, lace your fingers through his and swing your latched arms as you stroll. Couples don't hold hands anymore! Seriously, the next time you're out in a crowd of couples, notice how many of them hold hands as they walk. The numbers are so low that I always feel a little dorky when Jon and I do this while walking the dog or strolling to the grocery store. But then I remember that dorks are the new popular kids, and I keep holding on. We totally need to bring back that middle school display of affection.

2. Jump on his back. Nothing more fun and flirty than your man giving you a piggyback ride! Make him give ya one. If you can't hoist yourself up there anymore, don't despair. Try a mock piggyback when he's sitting on the couch. It's the wrapping yourself around him and holding on that's key.

3. Kiss loooooonger. I'm not talking about a "Get a room!" moment on the street. Although if you're into that sort of thing, have at it. I'm simply talking about a five-second rule for mouth mashing. Get rid of the little pecks and invest in a nice five-second lip lock. Mmmm . . . mmmmm . . . good. People won't tell you to get a room, you'll inspire them to get one of their own.

4. Compliment your partner in PUBLIC. I used to be neighbors with a girl who consistently, albeit jokingly, would make jabs at her husband and his ineptitude at social gatherings. She thought she was being hilarious. But everyone else just felt bad for her really-good-guy. Public displays of affection don't always have to be of the physical nature. Think of three things that you adore about your mate and tell them loud and proud the next time you're in a public forum. I'd like to take

this opportunity to tell Jon that he makes the best pancakes on the face of the planet, I think he's gotten even cuter with age, and his witty humor slays me every time.

5. Do something beyond cheeseball and embarrassing to show your undying L.O.V.E. I'm a sucker for those goofy lip-synch video proposals, and "We're knocked up!" announcements that go viral. But you know what? I want some shock and awww too! You don't have to record it and share with the world, but consider taking a page from the well-played romantics in your Facebook feed and do something unexpected and mortifying in the most sugary-sweet way possible, for all to see. Playfulness on point.

SUPER-SIZED YARD TWISTER

What You'll Need

* Old 5-gallon bucket
* Jigsaw or rotary saw
* String
* 2 stakes
* 1 (15-ounce) can each of red, blue, and yellow ground-marking spray paint
* 2 (11-ounce) cans of green ground-marking spray paint

Directions

1. Cut a roughly 7-inch diameter hole in the bottom of the bucket.

2. Select where in the lawn you want your Twister field. Pound in two stakes and run a string between them to make it easier to get the first row of paint circles straight.

3. Time to paint! Make the first row of circles red, the next blue, then yellow and green. Paint your first circle with the edge of the bucket touching the string; evenly space the rest of the circles.

4. You can make the Twister field as long as you'd like, depending on how many people will play at one time and how much ground marker paint you have to use. Have fun!

Reenact Some Sappy Rom-Coms

Dear men, standing outside our bedroom window with a boom box over your head playing "In Your Eyes" like John Cusack in *Say Anything* is (almost) equivalent to buying us a Chanel bag, getting up with the baby at 4:30 A.M., or doing the laundry . . . and putting it all away. Can you say #SureThing? I don't think you guys fully understand the significance of a really sappy romantic gesture. So let me enlighten you. We FREAKIN' LOVE THE SAP! Give us the SAP!!! We will eat that sticky stuff up and lick our fingers! I mean, we know you typically decide to do romantic stuff with the hope and dream of getting laid. (Don't tweet me, you know I'm right.) So when you do something platonically precious like serenade us in the front yard, write us a dorky love poem, or wrap your arms around us from behind while we're sitting at a pottery wheel (without touching our lady parts), it's like straight honey to the queen bee. Irresistibly delicious.

I have proof that these kinds of shenanigans will light your partner's fire. My adorable blogger friend Casey wrote a post over at YourTango about jumping into this idea with her own husband, and when I read it, my chick-flick-loving heart did somersaults out of my chest. After reading her post I actually Googled "how to do the movie-ending lift from *Dirty Dancing*." My husband is six-seven . . . I'll need some high-jump training. But it will be so totally worth it.

5 Romantic Comedy Moments to Re-Create for Yourselves

Now it's your turn!

Remember now, you get extra style points for embarrassment level, so please, don't take any of this too seriously. Just throw on some high-waisted khakis to help conjure up your inner Meg Ryan, and have at it. If you find yourself confused by any of the movie scenes listed below: Um, the interwebs. They will help you.

1. THE SLOW DANCING IN THE STREET MOMENT BETWEEN NOAH AND ALLIE IN *THE NOTEBOOK*. Just watch for cars.

....

2. THE POTTERY WHEEL MOMENT IN *GHOST*. No pottery wheel? No problem. Grab your kids' craft clay, put on some sexy music, wear a tank top, and make it up as you go.

....

3. THE *SAY ANYTHING* MOMENT WITH JOHN CUSACK, THE BOOM BOX, A TRENCH COAT, AND ANY SONG YOU WANT. Except "The Chicken Dance" or "I Want Your Sex."

....

4. THE AIRPLANE SCENE FROM *THE WEDDING SINGER* WHEN ADAM SANDLER SINGS TO DREW BARRYMORE THROUGH THE FLIGHT ATTENDANT MICROPHONE. If you can't clear it with TSA, create your own airplane . . . and mile-high club.

....

5. THE RIVERSIDE PARK SCENE AT THE END OF *YOU'VE GOT MAIL*. Plan a meeting time and place, and then act surprised to see each other and give him the Meg Ryan line: "I wanted it to be you. I wanted it to be you so badly." I mean . . .

Add a Little More "Fore" into Your PLAY

Before my husband and I were married, we fooled around a lot. We were YOUNG and waiting for the rings before hitting it all the way out of the park. But we knew how to "snuggle" really well.

What we learned from those early years in the dugout was that not all turns at bat need to lead to a triple home run. The pregame is often really underrated.

"Foreplay" at its core means "before play," before the big game or main event. But sometimes, it's fun to think of foreplay AS the main event. This can be hard for husbands, and maybe some wives, but seriously . . . husbands. I think I speak for most chicks when I say that when our batters take time to really stretch, take some time in the batter's cage just playing around, and linger at the bases a bit, before attempting to slide into home, we are more likely to give them the MVP award. And not all foreplay involves the actual "bases." I would not call my

husband a romantic. We will never be the couple who write each other poetry (unless it was slightly crude and Seussical), or do anything romantically serious, Zen-like, or meditative together. We once got kicked out of a couple's massage for laughing too much. We're just not that mature.

That said, there are lots of playful ways to warm up the field prior to the big game. Here are a few to bat around:

1. Fake a power outage. Turn off the lights, light all of the emergency candles, and aim to make out for no less than thirty minutes. Bonus points if you don't touch any naughty bits, and make it to forty-five.

2. Reminisce . . . half-naked. Flipping through old snapshots from your fledgling courtship and retelling stories from when you first fell in love is a playful way to sprinkle romance and sentimentality over your pregame show.

3. PILLOW FIGHT! (In your skivvies.) I recommend the use of a dimmer switch, and a glass of wine in the locker room before this activity. But no candles on the nightstand. Learn from my mistakes.

4. Read sappy poetry to one another. Okay, just because Jon and I are incapable of keeping a straight face in the presence of poetry readings doesn't mean you are. If you can

get away with writing or reciting your love a few playful and beautiful pieces of prose before jumping in the sack . . . game on! I applaud your class.

5. Fool around in your backyard.

All sexual metaphors and double entendres aside, the ability to playfully ~~hammer it home~~—sorry, I just can't help myself—the ability to really appreciate and amplify the built-in playfulness and teenage puppylove-ness of a romantic relationship helps to keep it new and exciting in the midst of all the monotonous and mundane that's bound to happen.

When's the last time you did something romantic and totally out of your "box"? (I did it again. My editor is going to kill me. . . . "This is a family book!")

Anyway, if you can't remember, it's time to put down the serious stick and pick up the playful one. And then take yourselves out to the ball game.

One of my favorite spiritual teachers and prolific writers, Rob Bell, recently collaborated with his wife on the book *The Zim Zum of Love: A New Way of Understanding Marriage*. Rob is a supercharged creative who sees the world and our human existence in the most mind-opening and truly delightful way. I asked Rob to share some ways he keeps his relationship with Kristen playful and fun.

Play Maker TILL DEATH DO US PLAY: 6 WAYS TO ADD PLAYFULNESS INTO YOUR MARRIAGE

Rob and **Kristen Bell,** bestselling authors
and motivational speakers

1. **Be rookies together.** Try something neither of you have done before, something you both know little about. Use new muscles, learn new skills, be first timers at it together. It's amazing how much life this can inject into the space between you. Take a class, try a new sport, create a project, make something together.

2. **Learn from the French.** Don't just dress up to go out on a date night once in a while, but add pleasure and flair to your daily life. Wear clothes that make you feel great (not yoga pants); have a "cocktail hour" where you tell the kids the two of you are spending some time catching up with a drink; enjoy good-quality, fresh food, even if just a small amount, like good chocolate or fresh strawberries; bring home something that says "I was thinking of you"; eat on the fine china.

3. **Music, music, music.** Few things add more electricity to the everyday moments of your life than music. Keep albums or playlists of songs in the kitchen that the two of you have enjoyed together over the years. This can add lightness and groove to those activities that can become a chore. And it may even lead to dancing.

4. **Develop inside language.** If you go to a restaurant and it takes forever to get a table and the service is terrible and the restaurant is called Jones's, then make that your new verb for

things not going well. Example: "We totally got Jonesed." No one will get it but you. And that's the point. You're creating your own little shared language, a secret only the two of you are in on . . .

5. **Be curious together.** Allow yourselves to be interrupted. If you're driving along and you see a store or market or open house or park you haven't seen before, pull over and check it out. Leave room in your schedule, and your life, to be surprised together.

6. **See the world.** Pick a place you've never been that you both want to visit and make a plan to go there together. Even if it takes a long time saving and planning, don't give up. The anticipation itself will make you feel like you're on an adventure together, let alone the experience and the shared memories you'll have.

Getting AFK'd! (Away from the Keyboard)

The case for looking up and getting down with each other more often.

How do we fully disconnect to reconnect? We all have tried to power down, stick our phones on their chargers, commit to going "off the grid" for the sake of our relationships, only to be magnetically pulled back to our devices, sneaking quick peeks under the table or in the bathroom while no one's looking. I've definitely used the "I have to pee" thing in order to make sure I'm not missing any comments I "need" to deal with on Facebook.

Get Yourself an Unplugged "Getaway" Place ... Without the Pesky Second Mortgage

One of the very best investments Jon and I have made over the last twenty-five years is our Michigan lake cottage, ninety minutes away. We didn't get that secret hideout until year twenty of twenty-five. But we've been "getting away" for many years.

When our first son, Maxwell, was very little we came up with a trick for feeling miles away from all of life's stress and mess. We lived in a condo in Chicago and there was not a ton of money for weekend babysitting. Since we just couldn't afford to go out every Friday night, we often played a silly game of imagining that our young parent pad was a jazz club in the city. We'd get Max down for the night, shut everything down, shake up some cosmos (thank you, *Sex and the City* . . . it was the late '90s; we were very trendy), light a ton of candles, turn on some Stacey Kent jazz standards, and pretend we had the club all to ourselves. The magic of make-believe should never grow up and move on just because we do. Put the kids to bed, pull all the plugs, set the scene (check Pinterest for theme ideas!), and GO there. With a touch of playful pretending, your house in the burbs can suddenly become an imaginary galaxy far, far away.

10 Places to Pretend Your Way into This Friday Night

* A stabbin' cabin (you be the "other" woman)
* A blues club
* A casita in Mexico
* A piano bar
* A ski chalet
* A café in Paris
* The Chateau Marmont in L.A. Look it up. My fav place to pretend I'm a celebrity.
* A campground . . . sleeping bags and tabletop s'mores, anyone?
* An ice castle right out of *Dr. Zhivago* . . . vodka, fur hats, and "Lara's Theme"
* A jazz club in NYC . . . my favorite land of make-believe

Keep Some Snaps to Yourselfie

Sneak away somewhere romantic and have a photo shoot built for two. And then DO NOT share them on any social media platforms. Even the really, really cute ones! Be strong, I know it's tempting!

We have become a social media–motivated society that now feels compelled to package and present every precious, private moment to the whole wide world. When I see families or couples taking photos with their smartphones, I instantly imagine what filter they'll use to photo edit the shot and whether it's going on Instagram, Facebook, or Twitter . . . or maybe all three at the same time! You know what's sexier than ever before? Privacy. Documenting moments exclusively for the two of you, totally secret from the rest of the world, shows your mate that his or her love and approval is all you're after. So grab your phone or a real live camera with actual film, and have a little photography session exclusively for your one most valued follower. PG or R rated is your call. As long as it's consensual, private, and you keep your coochie-coo off the Cloud, you're all good.

3 Easy Ways to Use Your Camera as a Flirtation Device

1. **SEXTING . . . SORT OF.** I am ALL for sending slightly racy snap shots to your significant other at work, when they're traveling, when they're out with the guys, or when they're sitting next to you on the couch and you want to get their attention. But a word of caution. Do NOT digitally send full-on nakedness across the clouds . . . big brother is eagerly watching.

And be sure your mate deletes such shots shortly after viewing, ESPECIALLY if you have the whole Apple TV setup that automatically displays ALL of the photos in your stream in a lovely montage on your home's flat-screen TV, to music, for the entire family to see. AWWWWK-ward.

2. **BE HIS MUSE.** As a blogger and "TV personality," I have been privileged to be a part of some very fun photo shoots where ya get all hair-and-makeupped and have a professional photog telling you how to "work it, work it" in front of the camera. There's something very playful and flirty about the whole

thing. Give your mate the opportunity to make you his muse. Let him be behind the lens and direct you as he clicks away. My husband once did this in a very tasteful way (all on his own), as I was slowly getting dressed one Saturday morning . . . with a VERY foggy filter, and the shots were so subtly sexy and artistic that we ended up getting one framed for his office! I still don't think the girls in his workplace know that it's me on his wall. But he does, and that's allll that matters.

3. **MAKE HIM YOUR MUSE.** Turn the tables and the camera on HIM and do the same thing. Be playful and fun with your shots; guys don't typically enjoy the duck-face model-posing thing. The key here is keeping everybody else out of your photo session. It may sound slightly basic, but in the land of the constant share, keeping moments to ourselves makes them feel significantly more special.

Play with

"A little nonsense now and then is cherished by the wisest of men"

- ROALD DAHL

Your

Friends

P eer playmates are an absolute must-have for a happy, healthy, well-played life. It doesn't matter how "busy," career driven, serious, antisocial, or introverted you think you are.

Play researchers (yes, they really are a thing!) have discovered over and over that human beings do best when they have regular doses of play in their lives. We also all need positive human connection to thrive and become our best selves. And studies show that humans positively connect like dot-to-dots when they are in the midst of a playful experience. With every giggle-ridden adventure, ridiculous escapade, or episode of fun and games we share with the folks we've chosen as our friends, the dots quickly connect, and the fuller friendship picture comes into view. Mine usually ends up looking like a unicorn pooping rainbows.

Well Played

In other words, playfulness makes us happier people.

Creating time to play with our personal tribe of carefully curated comrades is often on our "want to do" list, but can often seem completely frivolous and unnecessary. Not to mention that it also gets exponentially harder, the older and wiser we become, to find the time to play.

The "stuff" of life takes up a whole lot of time and energy. But if you think you don't really need to play, you're all kinds of wrong. The desire to play is a hardwired, innate drive that we simply never outgrow. The harder we run from it, the more our soul begs for its return. You may not recognize the unfulfilled, sad, depressed, or stifled feeling that results from a lack of play in your life, but research in brain development and play tells us to check there first.

Some of you might also believe that you just can't afford to play around. You've got work to do and a family to raise, and it can be expensive to fund the fun, right? Sometimes. But truthfully, many of the most playful experiences of my life have required little or no money at all. Ever play freeze-tag with your kids around the outside of your house? Exactly.

Don't get me wrong, it was thrilling to scuba dive in Grand Cayman, zip line in Mexico, and dog sled in Iceland (the Sinclairs are a traveling crew). But my kinds of daily doses of play most often require little more than an open mind, a playful spirit, and a keen sense of how to turn twenty minutes into something magical.

When it comes to playing with our pals, again, it's a matter of importance and priority. The same way that we gravitated toward, and held tight to those best buds of our childhood, so must we thoughtfully hunt and gather the BFFs of our grown-uphood.

If you have kids, then you're aware that there are often two kinds of parental pals: the ones we find ourselves sort of stuck with because our kids are friends with their kids, and the ones we, as I like to call it, double-click with from the moment we meet at the playground, work-

178

place, coffee shop, or carpool line. And if you're really lucky, there are girlfriends who land smack dab in the middle of this mom-friend Venn diagram.

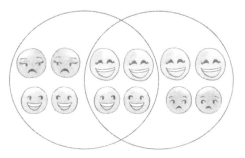

It's vital to find our posse, our crew, the folks with whom we can act ridiculous, get a little silly, and rest assured we won't be tagged in a grossly unattractive photo on Facebook. Remember . . . real friends add flattering filters. If you aren't lucky enough to already have a gaggle of girls to call your own, it's time you got on that.

I've moved several times, as my husband and I followed his TV producer career, hopping from market to market until finally landing in Chicago. And each time we landed in a new location, I had to find new friends to play with. Friend dating takes time, intention, and a simple yet effective game plan.

And now, after living in the same city for twenty years, I have a whole lot of friendly acquaintances but just a solid handful of really good friends. The ones I count on for last-minute adventures, deep emotional talks, and everything in between. I've intentionally curated a really good batch of playmates, and I love them dearly. A few had to be cut from the squad for personal foul penalties, and my "team" has definitely ebbed and flowed as my kids have grown and new players have shown up for practice, but consistently, there are at least five players I always have on my sideline.

The 5 Friends
Every Girl Needs in
Her Playgroup

If you have at least one of each of the following kinds of girlfriends, your personal playgroup is bound for success . . . and a whole mess of unabashed, good times. If you have more than one of each of these girls, you deserve a trophy. And not just for participation. For KILLING IT!

1. **THE FIRE STARTER:** This chick is your planner. She rallies the troops, sets actual dates and times for gatherings, sends out the invites, and feels at home hosting. She's your creative cruise director.

2. **THE "HELL YEAH!" GIRL:** Her FOMO usually gets the best of her and makes her a sure thing. She'll do almost anything once, loves an adventure, and RSVPs first to every invitation.

3. **THE SPARKLER:** Want to know the latest, most fun activity to do or try? Need a playful kick in the arse to get out and have a really good time? She's your girl. She's the vinegar to your baking soda, the match to your fire, the one who calls you up and leads with the question "You know what we should do!?"

4. **THE SPONTANEOUS COMBUSTOR:** You never know when she might call or show up at your doorstep asking if you can come out to play. She'll teach you the glory of leaving room for spontaneity and the opportunity to forget work, deadlines, dinner, bosses, tantrums, and to-dos, and just play hooky for a while.

....

5. **THE MESSY-HOUSE GUEST:** That friend for whom you never have to scramble to clean up your messy, playfully lived-in abode. She seriously doesn't give a hoot about the dishes in the sink, the toys all over the floor, or the baskets full of laundry that decorate your home. She's here to have fun, or just listen, and none of that matters one lick.

Coincidentally, as this book launches, I'll be moving across the country to Los Angeles, where I'll have to start this pal-search process allllll over again. Anyone know of a Match.com app for cool, ready-to-play friends?

YARD YAHTZEE

What You'll Need

* 6 squares for your giant dice (Wood works great. You can purchase a 4 x 4 from the hardware store and ask them to cut it for you. Foam is another option for smaller kids)
* Acrylic paint (the more colors the better!)
* Round sponge brush
* Sealant
* Yahtzee score sheets
* Plastic tub (optional)

Directions

1. Get your kids to help you paint the cubes. Let them pick out the colors for each die and have them paint all the sides of the cubes (you'll need to let some sides dry before painting the others).

2. Once all the paint has dried, use the round sponge brush to add dots to your die. Make sure to use a color that contrasts well.

3. When your dots have dried, use an outdoor sealant on all sides of the die. Because there may be strong fumes, this is a good steps for adults to do alone, preferably outdoors.

4. Once the sealant has dried, you're ready to play! Your kids can choose to roll each die singularly, or use a plastic tub to roll them all together. Yahtzee is a great way to work with kids on their math skills, especially during the summer. For younger kids who aren't quite ready for Yahtzee, try matching games.

3 Steps to Playing More with Your Own Friends

"Wasted" time gets a bad rap. I believe what we do with our "wasted" time says a whole lot about what we really would rather be doing, and what brings us fulfillment, relaxation, and joy.

1. **WASTE NOT, WANT NOT.** Clock your "wasted" time for seven days. I know all of you just yelled at this book, "I don't have any wasted time!" I get it: You're busy and productive every waking hour. But for one little week, throw me a bone and keep a simple log of the time you are spending on Facebook and Instagram being a voyeur of other people's fun and finding out what fruit best represents you, or clicking around the interwebs aimlessly, or flipping through your 327 cable channels of nothing special. Just log that time.

2. **REASSIGN YOUR WASTED TIME.** Now that you've taken a hard look at how you're spending your nonwork, responsibility-driven time, consider how you might be able to replace some of those minutes or hours with activities that will ignite your playful spirit.

3. **PERMANENT MARKER IT IN.** This is the fun part! Open up your weekly planner (I still use a paper one), and set up some playdates for you and your friends. Just do it! Try for one a week, biweekly, or once a month if that's all the wasted time you've

got. Most important, make it immovable. Sharpie that shizzle in! Enlist a group of pals who will go along with you on this "more play" adventure, and cast a wide net of playmates for your team. Life is unpredictable, and stuff will absolutely come up. Friends will cancel last minute, so plan accordingly. You'll quickly find out who wants to play and who's just not that into you and your shenanigans.

Make the First Move

Let's take a cue from Gandhi, who told us to be the change we want to see in the world. What goes for the whole wide world also goes for our own little patch of personal life. If you desire more playfulness in your own front yard, you're going to have to make it the greenest. In other words: Stop waiting for fun to miraculously land at your feet! Playfulness rewards the ones who go looking for it.

FRIENDSHIP BRACELETS FOR YOUR GROWN-UP BESTIES

Do friendship bracelets ever go out of style? Of course not. Wearing a small token of friendship is a great way to put some pep in your step. Although you can make bracelets alone, it's way more fun to gather up your besties for a DIY BFF Bracelet Night.

What You'll Need

* Leather lacing in a color of your choice
* Small brass hex nuts (about 20 per bracelet)
* Bracelet clasps

Directions

1. Cut your leather lacing into three strands that will wrap around your wrist twice. Knot the three pieces, including one side of the bracelet clasp.

2. Begin a simple braid with your leather and continue for a few inches.

3. To start adding the nuts to your bracelet, string a nut on the far left leather strand. Push the nut all the way up to the braid, then cross the leather over. Hold the nut in place with your thumb, and do the same steps on the right side.

4. Repeat until all nuts have been strung onto your bracelet.

5. Finish the rest of your bracelet with a plain braid. Add a knot and the other side of the bracelet clasp.

Field Trip Equality

Why should kids get all the field-trip fun? Bring back the joy of group exploration by mapping out a few months or even a year's worth of field trips for you and your best mates. Share the planning load by assigning various members of your group a month or season in which to organize a playful adventure. Your field trips don't have to be elaborate or expensive. Be a tourist in your own town or city, take a day trip in search of a new experience, or play together in your own backyards.

8 Field Trips to Slap on Your Schedule This Year

1. **IF YOU'RE LUCKY ENOUGH TO HAVE AN INDOOR TRAMPOLINE PARK,** go there with your grown-up pals. Consider it your cardio workout plus ridiculousness all bounced into one! If your town doesn't have one of these close by, A. I'm so sorry, and B. plan a jump fiesta just for grown girls at a friend's backyard tramp. Pro tip: If you've had children, empty your bladder before bouncing, and maybe pack a change of gutchies or a Depends undergarment. If you know, you know. It's so totally worth it!

2. **BOOK SOME TIME AT AN INDOOR OR OUTDOOR GO-KART TRACK** for your playgroup in the middle of the afternoon. Off hours + groups = discount rates. You won't believe how much you'll learn about your pals when you serve up a cocktail of power and speed with a slice of friendly competition.

3. **HIT AN AMUSEMENT PARK FOR A HALF DAY.** Do not tell your children. They can't handle the truth.

4. **CREATE A FIND-AND-SEEK GAME FOR A LOCAL ART OR HISTORY MUSEUM,** with clues or riddles of things to hunt down while you're there. I've done this with my kids, but it's equally fun with a batch of girlfriends.

5. **HEAD TO A NEIGHBORHOOD IN YOUR AREA, OR A PART OF YOUR OWN 'HOOD THAT YOU'VE NEVER EXPLORED, AND FIND THE MOST FUN THING TO DO THERE.** After living down the street from an astoundingly beautiful Baha'i temple, I recently took a field trip with a few friends to explore it together. It's amazing what we can overlook right in our own backyards, isn't it?

6. **FIND OUT WHERE YOUR LOCAL GIRL SCOUTS OR BOY SCOUTS GO FOR THEIR FIELD TRIPS . . .** and go there. Hiking, camping, white-water rafting? Yes, please. I've

often thought about creating a "Mom Scout Troop," complete with sashes and sewn-on badges. You want one too. I know it.

7. TAKE TURNS PLANNING "MY FAVORITE THING" FIELD TRIPS, introducing the group to something you love to do for fun. You'll be surprised how much you all learn about one another just by how you each like to play around. When in doubt, gather your best girls and hit any place your kids have been begging you to take them for their birthday parties. Why should our loveable little minions have all the fun?

8. HAVE A SNOWMOM-MAKING PARTY FOR YOUR BEST MATES. Make one big snowmom, or have everyone build her own, and then take a batch of selfies with your new frigid friends. Make sure you have a hot chocolate bar ready afterward with loads of toppings and a little Baileys ... it's good for the soul.

Go, Team!

Organized sports are not just for the youngsters in your life. Being a part of a team at any age is great for the mind, body, and spirit. My neighborhood fully gets it that grown-ups benefit from communal playtime as much as their kids, and is busting with opportunities for the adults to suit up and take the field as well. Check your local park district websites for opportunities to play with a batch of your girlfriends or mixed couples.

I have a friend, Laurie, who is the epitome of jumping in and playing big. She is the one you always want on your team, and she pretty much says "YES!" first to anything playful and fun. We all need folks like that in our tribes. She always makes me want to sign up for co-ed volleyball or doubles tennis.

Feeling like you could use a little team spirit in your life? Here are a few popular team sports with teams for us big kids:

1. PADDLE TENNIS: This outdoors, cold-weather game is a mash-up of Ping-Pong, racquetball, and tennis and is super popular in my Chicago suburb. It's the perfect antidote for the stuck-inside winter blues.
2. SOFTBALL: I've played as a sub for our community's co-ed team, and I shocked myself at my catcher abilities.
3. VOLLEYBALL: We have both beach volleyball and indoor volleyball teams for the parents in our village. Our neighborhood knows how to bring it at the net.
4. FLAG FOOTBALL: I've been wanting to form an all-girl team for years! How much fun would this be?! I think I'm going to ask a few husbands to coach and ref, and we'd be good to go.
5. WOMEN'S ICE HOCKEY: One of our local teams is called the Mother Puckers. I've considered joining just for the jersey alone.
6. BADMINTON: Believe it or not, this laid-back yard game can get ferocious in some necks of the woods.
7. SHUFFLEBOARD: My family is obsessed with table shuffleboard, which is making a huge comeback.
8. SOCCER: Dads have had leagues for years, and now the moms are catching up. We have mom teams for each of our town's elementary schools, and it's no joke. These ladies are badass. In a really good way.

Leave Room for "Last Minute"

This playful principle has taken a load of "unplanning" and practice for me to master. And I still don't have it totally down. Unplanned, spur-of-the-moment, throw-me-for-a-loop moments have not traditionally been my favorite fare. I like the predictable. Don't get me wrong. I like surprises too; I just like to know about them ahead of time.

It has taken a few spontaneity-loving pals (the best and closest Spontaneous Combustors) in my life to teach me that some of the most intoxicatingly playful episodes can show up when I least expect them. My friend Sari shows up on her bike at my front door and entices me to stop everything and go for a spin to the lake. My pal Lauri is a ringleader of fun and games, and often throws out the Bat-Signal of fun, texting to ask who wants to meet up and have a girls' night on a Wednesday. And then there's the other Laurie, who is almost ALWAYS the first friend to respond with an exuberant "I'm IN!" whenever I toss a crazy play plan out to my comrades. I love having pals like that in my posse. They're invaluable. Make sure you've got some too.

Running away to play at a moment's notice is not always practical or feasible.

But every so often, the call to play comes right out of nowhere, and right when I need it most. Folks like me and those with overstuffed schedules and planned-to-the-minute agendas have to intentionally leave patches of untethered space in our lives to allow Madame Spontaneity to show up. It really is a matter of practice makes perfect. So here's what I want you to do.

Pick a random weeknight or weekend morning, and rally your troops for a spur-of-the-moment playdate and see what happens. Once you throw a few of these sudden invites out there, your cronies will start to follow suit. You'll never regret leaving a smidge of room for last-minute frivolity within your get-it-done days. I promise.

Willie Geist, cohost of the *Today* show and *Morning Joe*

1. GO BIG. We fill our house to capacity with friends and family every weekend. We love mixing people from all corners of our life who may not have known each other, but are the best of friends by the time they pull out of the driveway on Sunday.

2. GET WEIRD. We have a giant closet full of costumes, instruments, and industrial-size karaoke equipment for both kids and grown-ups. But mostly for grown-ups, honestly. Our house is a judgment-free zone. Also, a social media–free zone.

3. APPOINTMENT HANG-OUTS. Make a tradition with friends to meet up somewhere away from home once a year. Pick somewhere fun, find a decent hotel, and spend a weekend doing what you love. For us, that's eating and drinking without our children. They're great, but . . . ya know.

4. RUNNING COMMENTARY. We all have friends across the country we don't see enough. One way to keep the spirit of the group alive is with a giant, running, always-open mass text chain. It's a big forum to keep up on everyone's families and jobs, and to gratuitously mock each other at any hour of the day.

5. CAMELOT. Play touch football in the yard of your oceanfront home, barefoot and wearing crisp white button-downs and chinos. Sorry, that's the Kennedys. The Geists play tackle.

Quilting Bees and Wannabes

As I've stated before, I'm not all that artsy or craftsy. But I'm a desperate "maker" wannabe, which is half the battle. I sometimes long for the days of sewing circles and quilting bees. I mean, those powwows must have been the ultimate "Kumbaya" of craftiness, no? I think there's real magic in a communal project. It makes the insecure learning curve for something you're not all that good at slightly less curvy. Especially if it involves a cocktail or two . . . sorry, prairie women, there are serious benefits to being born a little later on the timeline.

I first experienced the joy of joint craftiness when one of my creative pals, Ann Marie, invited me to a homemade paper-making lesson at a farm in Michigan, where we learned the pulp-to-papyrus process from a master artist. I never would have thought to plan that experience for myself, but it was invigorating to learn something so out of my regular toy box, and to play in a whole new way.

If you don't have a friend who plans cool stuff like that, no worries. They're all around you. Creative shops like Paper Source and Michaels craft stores offer loads of fun and inexpensive seasonal classes. Even if those don't sound like your cup of tea, sign yourself and a few friends up, and see what happens. Getting lost in the act of playful creation is good for your brain, body, and soul.

COLORING PARTY: GROWN-UPS ONLY!

This idea comes from the awesome Katherine McHenry, the owner of Building Blocks toy store in Chicago. Coloring books are all the rage right now, so why not have a coloring party with your girlfriends? You can find adult coloring books in most craft stores and bookstores these days, and I highly recommend splurging a few dollars on some fine-tip markers or colored pencils instead of digging through your kids' box of broken crayons. Have everyone over for a friends' night, and ask them to bring a coloring book or two and their coloring utensil of choice. Then gather around a table to share colors and stories. Adult beverages optional, but highly recommended.

Mom Movie Nights: A Total Must-Do

I have become semi-famous among dozens for my every-so-often Mom Movie Nights. They're a "thing" I'm kind of known for, and it almost makes me more excited than being recognized from my *Today* show segments. Almost. Ever since my days as an elementary classroom teacher, I've loved a good thematic unit. Themes are obnoxiously fun. I love them.

So now that I'm no longer creating units for second-grade math and science, I've transferred that creative energy into my movie nights. I have an up-for-anything core group of girls I know will show, as well as new pals that I add to the mix now and again. We've watched

Sixteen Candles for back-to-school with custom cocktails, Mad Libs, and "school pictures" (set up a fun backdrop, add some silly school-related props and a digital camera on a tripod, and you're set!).

We've viewed *Meatballs* at the start of summer-camp season, with blankets and sleeping bags on the floor and campy fare, and we've had a *Xanadu* screening (remember that musical-meets-magical cult classic?), complete with disco balls, rainbow tats, and a surprise magician. Putting these together feeds my playful creativity, and the end result is a night of being teenagers again—and that beats any book club.

Here are five movie night themes to get your own movie nights off the ground and onto the big screen. Please note that you do not need to have produced a child to become famous for these epic movie nights. I call them "Mom Movie Nights" because my friends are pretty much all moms. Call them anything you want!

5 Mom Movie Nights Your Pals Will LOVE

PRETTY IN PINK: Show this flick around prom season, have your pals dress up in vintage (aka Goodwill) prom dresses, bring their prom photos to share, serve punch and cookies, and play a game of "Brat Pack" trivia.

ELF: If you don't like this holiday comedy, we can't be friends. Make this a dessert party, serving all things sugar ... Buddy the Elf's favorite. Put together a simple but elegant hot cocoa bar on a bar cart or prettied-up card table, make celebrity naughty and nice lists, and have your besties wear their favorite holiday jammies.

SEX AND THE CITY: Go all NYC-themed for this girls' night in. Serve cosmos (of course), have a *Sex and the City* trivia contest, give your girls Manolo Blahnik stiletto coloring pages so they can design their own pair, and chow down on Chinese takeout.

. . . .

BREAKFAST AT TIFFANY'S: Deck your place in classic Tiffany blue, hand out party store tiaras, create a simple photo booth (you can get *Breakfast at Tiffany's*–themed photo props on Etsy for six bucks!), have your girls wear LBDs, and serve blue cocktails. Check out Pinterest for more ideas!

. . . .

BIG: Pull out some of the classic toys of your youth, like Lincoln Logs, Colorforms, Slinkys, Shrinky Dinks, and Simon, and encourage your pals to play a little. Make paper "fortune tellers," serve cotton candy and other carnival food, and if you have a trampoline, hit the backyard after the movie for some grown-up bouncing.

. . . .

FROZEN: Just kidding.

. . . .

BIG TIP! Avoid asking your girlfriends what they want to watch for movie night. You'll quickly find yourself in a merry-go-round of C-SPAN-esque debate and rebuttal. Just pick one and go with it.

. . . .

Grown-Up Game Night

Everyone is too busy and stressed for a night of playing around—making it even more of a must-do for you and your friends. Think of it as preventive health care. Laughing regularly extends your shelf life. Look it up. It's also remarkably good for your stress level and emotional well-being.

So instead of another dinner-and-a-movie night, or an evening sipping drinks in a sports bar, invite your cronies over for some healthy and hilarious competition. Some of your "I hate games" acquaintances may run the other way, but I promise that if you can get them in the door, they'll love every goofy minute.

Not sure which games will make your grown-up gathering the most fun? Here are a batch of my own and my Facebook friends' favorites.

* Heads Up
* Catch Phrase
* Hollywood Game Night
* Cards Against Humanity: so wrong, so funny
* Apples to Apples
* Guesstures
* Telestrations
* Celebrity
* Logo
* Balderdash
* Strike a Pose
* Spit It Out
* Crappy Birthday
* Spoons
* Scattergories
* Wise and Otherwise
* Never Have I Ever
* 5 Second Rule
* Reverse Charades
* Loaded Questions
* The Game of Things
* What's Yours Like?
* Taboo
* Imaginiff
* Jenga (add cocktails and it's super challenging)

Over the course of the last fifteen years in our suburban neighborhood, I've been a part of many game nights with my pals. For a while we had a bimonthly "game group" of about six couples. We took turns hosting game nights in our homes, with the host couple getting to pick the games we played. Mixing up husbands and wives on separate teams is some of the most hilarious fun around. Or an episode of *Maury*. Like a '70s key party without the naughty bits, and a whole different kind of embarrassment the next day.

My husband and I have also held semiannual sleepover shuffleboard tourneys at our lake house for our favorite couple friends. We make the couples split up and pick someone else's spouse to be their teammate. My husband ALWAYS prays to be Laurie's partner because she's pretty much good at everything. EVERYTHING. And she always looks beautiful kicking your ass in any competition as well. Thankfully I adore her too, so there is no jealousy. Hell, I would pray to be her partner too.

The only tricky bit about hosting a game night is the folks who believe they totally HATE, with a capital H, playing games. You may be one of those people. Not everyone enjoys the stuff that comes with a group game night. The competition, the chaos, the having to be all "out there" and vulnerable. Let's face it: You've got to be willing to look a little foolish in front of your peers. I would actually pin my husband as a hater of sorts. He calls the Midwestern card game euchre "puker" and has told me he'd rather stick a fork in his eye than play Pictionary. So there's that.

But I also have seen said haters, when given a slight nudge and a healthy cocktail, become some of the biggest pigs in the playful puddle.

If it's been a long long long time since you've busted out the game boxes and bellied up to the board, give it a go! Just make sure you pick Laurie for your team first.

Make Beautiful Music Together

The music shop in my village is called The Rock House, and along with giving loads of lessons to bunches of kids, it also offers classes like "Soccer Mom to Rocker Mom," ukulele classes just for the grown-ups, and open-mic nights where all are welcome to jump onstage and give it

a go. I once sang Fleetwood Mac's "Landslide" accompanied by a very talented real-musician girlfriend of mine. It was slightly terrifying and completely exhilarating.

If you're nervous to take music lessons on your own, do it with friends. If you gather enough friends, you can probably persuade your local music shop to give you a group lesson.

Creating music together (no matter how primitive) shreds our adult inhibitions into little pieces, and (if we allow it to) can re-ignite those latent five-year-olds in all of us who sang at the top of their lungs in the grocery store for all to hear, or composed original scores with wooden spoons and their mom's pots and pans.

Beyond the Book Club

I have nothing against a book club. Really, I don't. It's just that the ones I've been a part of became more about drinking wine and gossiping about the neighbors than about the actual book. If you're in a book club that you're loving, high five! Well done. But if you're not, I implore you to stop cramming the book the night before, and start a new kind of club.

Two of my best gal pals told me about a group they used to be a part of called The Gathering. Each month, they would pick a theme or topic, like "favorite magazine article you've read this month" or "best dessert I've ever made" or "tricks I use to get my kids to stay in their bed." Then each person prepares something to share on that topic.

I think this idea is perfection.

Kudos to all of you who are in book groups, actually finish the chosen book on time, and then refrain from spending your entire group time talking about your kids or gossiping about the other moms in the 'hood instead.

But I'm a girl who likes to take two months to read an Elin Hilderbrand book, slowly savoring all the angst-ridden relationship-ness of it. Plus, I find time to read only in bed at night and usually make it through about five pages before drifting off. The idea of having to read only a magazine article or prepare a recipe to share is right up my short-attention-span alley. And leaves plenty of time to talk only GOOD gossip about the other moms in the 'hood.

Run Away Together

Whether near or far, there is absolutely nothing like a little (or big) "girls' trip" with your favorite females to jump-start your playful engine. It doesn't have to be an over-the-top, expensive journey to a far-off land. It doesn't have to be for a whole week or involve costly plane tickets. Just slipping away for a night or two with the sole purpose of playing together is truly priceless. Book a couple of rooms at a local hotel, camp out together, or drive to a nearby town and shack up in an Airbnb rental.

I love having a group of gals up to our family's lake cottage in Michigan for an overnight of unplugged playtime. No phones, TV, Internet, or work allowed. We isolate our estrogen, get giddy, and act fifteen again. The trampoline and the zip line are the crowd favorites. Have I told you enough how much I LOVE jumping on a trampoline? Jumping with your kids and jumping with your own friends are two very different kinds of ridiculousness. You'll laugh and giggle jumping with your kids. You will pee your pants and get laughter-induced stomach cramping when jumping with your adult friends. But friends laugh with you, not at you, so jump away!

Stand Up

This one is all about the power of a really profound belly laugh. The first time my husband and I went to see a comedy show together, we turned to each other a couple of minutes in with a look that bellowed: "WHY haven't we ever done this before?" Collective laughing is like a shot of happy right to the soul. We have the world-renowned Second City here in Chicago, plus loads of comedians who stop here on tour. We're lucky like that. But I've seen horrible comics in Cocoa Beach and had just as much fun. Instead of the same old girls' night in, grab some tickets to the local laugh factory and lose yourselves in LOLs.

Scare Yourselves Silly

If there is something you've always wanted to do, but you're simply too chicken to go it alone, make it a playdate for you and your girls. Skydiving, bungee jumping, white-water rafting, surfing, trapeze tricks, mechanical bull riding, or any other *Fear Factor*–like activity is more palatable with pals. Adrenaline is a powerful chemical, and it's fun to get it pumping through your veins, but it's also nice to hold someone's hand when you're facing your fears.

Last year, I participated in a social media/photography conference that was held over a seven-day Caribbean cruise (bloggers know how to roll work into play really well). One of our day trips was to the Atlantis resort in the Bahamas. My colleagues and I spent the day at the resort laughing our way down the not-so-lazy river, zipping down the water slides, and contemplating the massive, scary-as-hell, straight-down flume named the Leap of Faith.

I'm a pretty gutsy girl, but this thing gave me pause. I wanted to run at it and hide from it all at once. I decided I had nothing to prove and that I'd pass on this one—until five minutes before the bus was about to take us back to the ship. As we were about to board the bus, I turned to my adventurous friend Rachel (who was also being a scaredy-cat) and quickly blurted out, "If you go on that terrifying slide, I will!" We took a deep breath, grabbed hands, and ran to the slide as fast as our middle-aged mom feet could carry us. Rachel and I talked ourselves in and out of going through with it all the way up the endless stairs to the top. And then, to save us from the embarrassing walk back down those stairs, she and I both threw our bodies down that water-filled skyscraper, screaming like happy idiots the whole way down. It was a highlight of the whole darn trip.

Planning a playdate that fully challenges your mild fears and inhibitions is often best done with a loyal pal. One who, in the retelling of the story, will always make you look braver than you were.

Play Makers 5 WAYS WE TURN WORK INTO FUN AT COOL MOM PICKS

Liz Gumbinner and **Kristen Chase**,
publishers/cofounders at Cool Mom Picks

1. LOVE WHAT YOU DO. Of course this isn't an option for everyone. But if you can find some way to wake up each morning, excited to do whatever it is you do, it certainly makes the day more fun than sitting and counting the minutes until you can go home. Oh wait . . . we are home most of the time. Wow, we just realized we never actually leave work, and we're still having fun. That's pretty amazing! Whoo!

2. FACE TIME: REAL AND VIRTUAL. When you run an online business with staff working remotely, it's so important to be able to connect face to face. We may laugh at each other's emails and texts (and naughty emoji sentences, ahem), but there's nothing more fun than actually being together. So we're always sure we make time to see each other, whether it's a weekly video chat, or a senior staff offsite in Las Vegas. Pro tip: You can't not have fun in Vegas when you're with fun people. Even sober. Yes, for real.

3. MAKE YOURSELF LAUGH. We once published a headline for a new nursing bra that read, "Lift Them Up Where They Belong." We have no idea if it makes anyone else laugh, but if it makes us laugh, we're running it. Which is also why we love writing posts like the funniest cards for Mother's Day. You just can't go wrong with a good sperm-and-egg joke for mom.

4. CONFERENCE CALLS WITH CELEBRITIES. SORT OF. You know how before a conference call, there's a recording that asks you to state your name before being connected? Kristen said "Miley Cyrus" right after some ridiculous thing she was in the news for, and we all started the call laughing so hard, we could hardly speak. Thus began a new Cool Mom Picks tradition. Now there's huge pressure to come up with the best possible made-up name before any call and the bar is getting pretty high.

5. CAT VIDEOS. Seriously. Sometimes you just need to interrupt the never-ending flow of work-related emails, client demands, and emergency requests by sending your coworker a link to some random, laugh-out-loud YouTube video or Internet meme, whatever it may be. It can change the whole direction of your day.

Play It Forward

It's important to play well with others, and just as important to play well FOR others. A quick survey of your local community will reveal lots of ways you and your pals can combine fun with philanthropy. Over the years I've trained for and run charity 5Ks, packed care packages for the homeless, cleaned up city playgrounds, and been a part of many a charity event, all done with friends in tow. It's true that many hands make light work, and that work is made even lighter when it's done for others with some great playmates alongside you.

Consider scooping up some sisters once a month or seasonally, and playfully pitching in. You'll feed your playful spirits and your local community.

1. Walk dogs for the local animal shelter.

2. Tidy up the beach or bike path.
3. Get your tribe and train together for a 5K, raising big cash for a cause close to your hearts.

4. Refurbish your local playground or help build a new one (check out kaboom.org for more information on how to make this happen).

5. Collect lightly used games for a homeless shelter or children's hospital, and then play together. I take all of my extra toy and game samples from TV segments to a children's shelter in my community, and their joy is palpable.

6. Say yes to chaperoning school dances, going on the field trip, or signing up for lunch duty. But whenever possible, try to do these with your favorite friends. Things just got fun.

7. Paint your elderly neighbors' fence, or help them plant flowers in their yard.

8. Sing to and rock sick babies in the NICU.

9. Gather girlfriends and collectively cook a week's worth of meals for a friend who is in the trenches of newborn-hood or an illness.

10. Make friends with your local librarian and ask about starting a free story time for the little ones in your 'hood. This is especially great as your own kids get older and outgrow listening to you read aloud. I could read *Swimmy* out loud every day of my life.

Come from a Place of "Yes, And"

One of the core games of theatrical improvisation is called "Yes, and." It's a technique for working through an improvised scene where actors acknowledge what's been said and then add another thing onto it. The unpredictable silliness of an improv class makes it the perfect playdate for a group of your closest friends. You'll be vulnerable and embarrassed and laugh yourself into an ab workout.

Party Like It's 1949

The table games of our mothers' and grandmothers' generations are increasingly growing in popularity. Apparently just as old-lady names like Mabel, Olive, and Pearl are considered ultra hipster, so are old-lady games. And if they haven't hit your neck of the woods yet, you can be the trendsetter amongst your peeps.

My friend Sari recently told me about a new mah-jongg group for moms that's got a wait list and is all the rage in our little village. She's promised to take me to the next meeting. The whole thing feels very underground and exclusive, which makes it even more alluring. With all of us so digitally oversaturated, these types of convivial games are bringing back a sense of one-on-one sociability.

Tired of playing words with no friends? Give one of these a go instead! Learning to play some granny games just might put a spring in your step. Step-by-step directions can be found on the interwebs, but I advise having an older, wiser "gamer" teach you.

1. Mah-jongg
2. Bridge
3. Gin rummy
4. Backgammon
5. Bingo
6. Euchre
7. Hearts
8. Spite and Malice

Sprinkle ALL Your Parties with Pops of Playfulness!

I adore a girlfriend gab-athon over festive cocktails and yummy fare, where everyone opens up, lets their guards down, and connects over deep conversation. As women, we especially enjoy that kind of female hang time. We're talkers, most of us.

But too often, this kind of "spirit"-driven soiree seems to be our only M.O., our no-brainer, go-to way of gathering. I'm not saying that I don't deeply enjoy a good bottle of wine with my girls, but I am getting a teensy bit "over" feeling the NEED to imbibe in order to really have fun and connect with my tribe. I've discovered that sprinkling a few pops of playfulness into a women-and-wine fest creates a fun milieu that's ripe for creative and coherent connection. Try adding a little more play to your Pinot Grigio.

19 Playful Additions for Your Next Soirée

1. A makeup artist to teach everyone the perfect cat-eye look
2. A game of truth or dare
3. A small karaoke machine in the corner—they're irresistible
4. Download Dubsmash and use it. And then die laughing.
5. A DIY photo booth. Minted.com and Paper Source make this easy.
6. Temporary tattoo "jewelry"
7. Fill Super Soakers with paint, set up easels in the backyard, and shoot some masterpieces onto white canvas.
8. Disco balls
9. Hula hoops
10. A mixologist to come and teach the girls how to make a new cocktail
11. A Pinterest challenge: Provide supplies for your girls to make something difficult you found on Pinterest. The biggest fail wins!
12. A Twister mat and slippery socks

13. Sparklers
14. A hip-hop instructor for one hour
15. A tabletop Ping-Pong set for the dining room. Move over, appetizers.
16. Celebrity tabloid magazines, glue sticks, and the charge to create the most ridiculous collage in the room
17. Silly String
18. Stick-on mustaches for instant immaturity
19. A Polaroid instant camera. (They're back!) Put away your phones and have an old-school photo shoot.

SPIRIT ANIMAL DRINK STIRRERS

What You'll Need

* Small plastic animal toys, one for each of your friends (2 inches or so)
* Plastic stir sticks
* Electric drill and 7/64-inch drill bit (if you don't have one at home, most hardware stores will rent you one)
* Food-safe spray paint in a fun color
* Glue (optional, for extra hold)

Directions

1. Have your friends over to do this project together. Have them each choose their "spirit animal" to create their own drink stirrer (and maybe an extra to take home!).

2. Drill a hole in the bottom of each plastic creature where you'll put the stirrer.

3. Use the food-safe spray paint to coat your spirit animal in a playful color. You can also paint the sticks if you'd like. If you're unable to find food-safe spray paint, ONLY paint your tiny animal toy, and not the stick. I recommend giving everything a day to dry before using your stirrers in a drink.

4. Keep each of your friends' spirit animal stirrers in a fun glass at your home, ready for use whenever they stop by for a drink or two.

ART AND WINE NIGHT

What You'll Need

* Small canvases (one for each guest)
* Watercolor paints
* Paintbrushes
* Cups for water
* Cups for wine (very important to keep separate from your water cups)

Directions

Paint nites have become the go-to for girls night out lately. But why not have the same fun at home and save a couple bucks? Visit your local art supply shop and pick up some paints and small canvases. Then invite your friends over, pop open a bottle, put on your fave playlist, and paint the night away.

My hope is that the ideas I've described here have sparked in you the desire to shut this book, call your crew, send out the Bat-Signal of fun, and set up some much-needed playtime all your own. Developing, nurturing, and maintaining solid friendships is just as vital for our grown-up well-being as it is for our children. And the more playful we can make those friendships, the better. Playful experiences help to unlock that joy-filled, uninhibited, child-like vault we all possess.

Every girlfriend I have quickly lights up when talking about their elementary school, high school, or college besties, and all of the adventures and shenanigans they had with them when they were young and free. I believe those friendships of old are so precious in large part because they were smothered in playfulness. Carefree, unadulterated, daring fun, all at a time when we were figuring out who we were and who we wanted to be.

The great news is that although we are a little older and wiser, and may have mostly figured out who we want to be (at least for now), with a slight shift in habit and a little playful planning, that same delight and friend-filled joy is ours for the taking.

Now go call one of your own friends and ask them to come out to play!

Play for

Yourself

"She had a lively playful disposition that delighted in anything ridiculous"

— JANE AUSTEN

Remember that Ralph Waldo Emerson quote I shared with you earlier in the book about what a "happy talent" it is to know how to play? Let's revisit that for just a moment, shall we?

If I were a tattoo-gettin' kinda girl, I'd totally get those ten words inked down the inside of my forearm for sure. They remind me that playfulness is a gift. A talent that reaches its fullest potential with regular and intentional practice.

And while the ability to know how to play is a happy talent indeed, I think the ability to play by yourself, purely for the sake of your own personal fulfillment, just may be the happiest talent of all. Playing alone is simply the most perfect way to discover who you truly are, what makes your heart sing, what fills you up and sets you free, apart from anyone else's rules, judgments, or expectations.

When we become lost in a ridiculous or purely playful experience, we invite the stripping away of some of the stifling self-prescribed titles, roles, and overly grown-up responsibilities that are often yucking our yum.

Your playful spirit does not give even one rat's ass if you're now a CEO, Ph.D., M.D., LLC, D.A.D., or M.O.M. When it comes to our ego's effect on playfulness, size totally matters. If you want to be well played, you're aiming for the smallest one you can manage.

Play's not-so-secret mission is to return us to our truest, most joyful selves, unleashing the superpowers found in goofing off. Play has the ability to do that more perfectly than nearly anything else I've ever witnessed.

The beautiful act of playing all by ourselves isn't about pleasing or impressing our kids, our mates, or our best friends. It's not concerned with Facebook likes, audience applause, social media fame, or shiny trophies.

But permitting ourselves to stomp on the pause buttons of our overoccupied lives, look inward, and become deeply submerged in a personal pond of playfulness can be unreasonably challenging for many of us with big, grown-up lives. We are a hive of busy little bees. And busy is one big fat play killer.

Every day I sit with my coffee and create a laundry list of things I aim to accomplish by bedtime. Things to do to satisfy everyone in my life: my children, my husband, my editors, my segment producers, my friends, my dog.

Until I intentionally made space for myself on that list each day in the form of just one playful escape, I would fall into bed each night feeling completely emptied, disappointed, frustrated, and anxious about the next day. Because there were always stragglers left on my list, and I was having no fun at all.

I've come to discover that the whole work/play balance thing is like an old-school seesaw . . . the ones from back in the day with splintery wooden planks, very few safety measures, and an unpredictable balancing system. To really enjoy the full ride, we must be willing to take turns being down on the ground, stable and sure, and up in the clouds wild and free. If we don't balance life's stress-inducing workload with its happiness-producing playload, our inner teeter-totter will be fully off its rocker. You don't want to be off your rocker, now do you? Didn't think so.

Let's be pimps of playfulness rather than dealers of drudgery, whadda ya say?

Ready to get after it?

Creating a Personal Play Profile

What really lights you UP?

What makes you sparkle and wiggle with giddiness and delight?

When does your inner eight-year-old sing at the top of its lungs without a care for who's listening?

When are you wholly lost in the land of free play solely for your own benefit?

What connects you most purely to the play-FULL-est part of yourself?

Do you have a clue?

Have you forgotten where you've hidden the key to your personal bouncy house?

Just want a few more literal LOLs in your life?

Do you have any idea where your inner child is?

No?

Creating your "Personal Play Profile" is the first golden step on the yellow brick road to a well-played life. Take ten minutes to reconnect yourself to the happy talent that makes you forget for a moment what time it is, where your phone is, whose mother you are, and the fact that you have a million and one big-girl responsibilities.

My Personal PLAY Profile

Before you begin, find a comfortable, quiet, and mindful spot. Sit down, take a few deep breaths, and sink into yourself. You deserve the next twenty minutes.

Now, take a moment to reflect and answer the following questions:

1. WHEN YOU WERE A CHILD, WHAT WERE YOUR FAVORITE WAYS TO PLAY? CLOSE YOUR EYES AND PICTURE YOURSELF IN THE MIDST OF SOME OF THOSE PLAYFUL EXPERIENCES.

....

....

....

2. HOW ARE YOU FEELING JUST THINKING ABOUT THESE EXPERIENCES? WHICH EMOTIONS RISE TO THE SURFACE?

....

....

....

3. WHEN WAS THE LAST TIME YOU HAD THE SAME KINDS OF FEELINGS? WHAT WERE YOU DOING?

....

....

....

4. WHAT CURRENT ACTIVITY OR EXPERIENCE
BRINGS YOU CLOSE, OR RIGHT UP TO, THAT SAME
FEELING OF UNABASHED PLAYFULNESS YOU EXPE-
RIENCED AS A YOUNGSTER?

....

....

....

5. WHEN WAS THE LAST TIME YOU WERE WHOLLY
LOST IN A PURELY PLAYFUL EXPERIENCE JUST FOR
YOURSELF?

....

....

....

Now, list five ways you would LOVE to run away and play . . . especially if no one was watching, judging, or posting it on social media.

1. ....

2. ....

3. ....

4. ....

5. ....

Finally, pick one from your list and pop it into your planner this week!
Go. Now. Do it!

Bonus points: After you've completed three of the playful activities on your list, use the space below to describe how these experiences made you feel . . . mind, body, spirit.

....

....

....

....

....

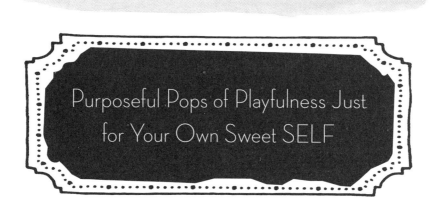

Purposeful Pops of Playfulness Just
for Your Own Sweet SELF

Ignore the Playground Rules

Playgrounds usually post strict age limits, and keep-out warnings for
grown-ups without kids. But when it comes to play, I think some rules

and restrictions are meant to be gently bent and occasionally straight up broken.

Of course, it would be quite alarming to see a pack of middle-aged men jump out of a minivan and run for the swings, or spend their lunch hour hanging from the monkey bars, knocking unsuspecting toddlers to the wood chips. Certainly older kids and adults should be respectful of little people's play spaces, and we need to keep creepy folks out. I get why the rules exist.

I'm aware. Playgrounds should always be safe.

What I am proposing is that we shift the way we grown-ups view these ultimate patches of playfulness. If you're a parent with playground-obsessed youngsters, I'm particularly talking to you.

Do you have a hate-hate relationship with the playground? Come on now, fess up.

I was recently taken aback a little by a friend's Facebook post confessing how much she literally **HATED**, in bold caps, spending time at the playground with her daughter. She said her daughter really didn't need or want her as a playmate and that consequently she felt trapped and bored, and pretty much loathed every minute. And she wasn't alone.

Mom after mom started climbing up her FB wall to share their own deep-seated dislike of "being trapped" at the playground as well.

I have to say I was dumbfounded. I honestly was fascinated and curious about what was causing such revulsion. I wondered if all this playground-hate was happening because the parents' grown-up responsibilities, work deadlines, and serious business rendered them unable to take a beat and envelop the fleeting magic and unstructured, goal-free play happening in that place.

Some moms mentioned that their kids also just didn't need or really want them to play with them anymore and said that they were painfully bored and resented having to hang there with "nothing to do."

You should know that I ADORE and very highly respect the mom who started it. She's an amazing mom, very involved with her daughters, and an inspiration in many ways. And because I love her, I was sitting there hollering at the screen, "Oh my GAWD . . . get up and play! Get up and play by yourself! Put down your phone and digital to-do list, and belly up to the monkey bars! For the love of Pete, get the heck off the bench and give a fist bump to the part of yourself that used to LOVE that place! I promise your beautiful inner child is curled up waiting just below your too-hip-to-skip facade . . . Go! Go and play with HER!"

The playground confessional also made me want to tell them how much paper money I would pay to be able to give my now teenaged boys one more under-dog on the swings, or to chase them across the shaky bridge and down the slide a few more times, or to sit on a swing of my own and simply watch them play with their friends for twenty minutes.

But I didn't say that. I didn't say any of that.

The playground hate-apalooza had picked up momentum, her FB

wall was flowing with slide shaming, and I just didn't want to sound preachy or Mary Poppins–esque. So I said nothing.

But this is my book, so I'm saying it now.

If you're sitting at a playground and feeling trapped and loathsome and bored, it's your own fault. You're throwing away a perfectly good bowl full of play-based JOY! Snap out of it!

Your kids love to see you play, for yourself, even when they don't "need" you to be their playmate anymore.

Be your own damn playmate! It shows them how to be their own.

Being grumpy at the playground is like going to a five-star restaurant that specializes in bacon-topped everything while you're on a juice cleanse. So sad.

This isn't about mom guilt or the notion that we should all be playing with our children nonstop, helicoptering over them, being their constant companions.

Nope, not at all.

But if you're the lucky one who gets to take your kid to the playground, allow yourself to be pleasantly surprised by the experience. Give yourself permission to jump off the to-do train and become playfully present not only for your kid, but for yourself!

What if you shifted your point of view and sought out ways to make your time at the playground a bit more of a mind-blowing, mood-boosting break for yourself as well? What would that look like for you? I'm talking about only an hour out of your day or week.

Imagine.

How to Make the Playground Your B*#CH

* Bring along a book and read on the swings or under a shady tree.

* Create a playground playlist for those times you just can't bear the other parents' small talk. It's okay.

* Grab a swing and pump up high because it swells your own heart.

* Scale that climbing wall because it makes you feel like you're ten years old again.

* Take a spin on that spring-bottomed unicorn because it's ridiculous and inappropriate, and your kids will think you hung the ever-loving moon.

* Embrace the Zen enlightenment of pushing your kid on the swings. Some parents apparently find this task excruciating. I think it's a brilliant session of calm the "F" down. The back-and-forth rhythm of a swing is alluring to your kids for a reason. It's like Xanax hung from two chains. It can be meditative, if you let it.

* Grab a blanket, a blank journal, some brightly colored fine-tip markers, and doodle, sketch, mind-dump, or write a more-fun manifesto!

* Coordinate with one or two of your favorite parental pals to meet you at the playground so you have someone to play with. This avoids having to pick up new mom pals at the monkey bars.

* Use it to friend-date! Single folks have Tinder; parents have the playground. If you're actually in the market for some new friends or you're new to the neighborhood and need a good place to hunt and gather like-minded cronies, the monkey bars is your Match.com. You can tell a lot about people by how they handle themselves in the sandbox.

Going It Alone

Sometimes I hit my neighborhood playground on evening dog walks when no one is there, taking a quick spin on the swings or a slip down the slide for no one's benefit but my own.

It feels borderline crazy and blatantly immature, and I usually laugh. Out loud. And then I laugh at myself for laughing out loud, which starts the whole thing in motion all over again. Sometimes crazy feels really good.

Running around a playground with my pooch or having a solo swing session and not posting it on Instagram or telling anyone about it feels freeing and privately playful, which is rarer these days than ever. Not everyone needs to see all of our fun and games.

Think of your local playground as a shot of happy juice at the end of a long day when tequila's not an option (playground therapy should totally be a "thing").

If you're thinking you would NEVER conduct yourself in such a manner, then you need a class in grown-up playgroundology. Try playing alone sometime. It may feel unbearably awkward at first, but give it a beat. I promise, you'll love it.

If you have older kiddos in your life and sadly believe that your playground days are over, you'd be wrong there too. Let me introduce you to a little something I like to call "The Art of Playground-Punking Your Unsuspecting Teenagers." Come along . . .

Try this maneuver when you're certain aliens have abducted your beautiful child and replaced him or her with an unrecognizable pre-pubescent extraterrestrial. It happens to the best of them. Not to worry.

With time and practice, and this five-step program, you too can make teenage grumpitude and snarkiness practically disappear!

STEP 1. When the haze of adolescent angst and reality show drama begins to choke out all goodness and light, get everyone's arse in the car.

STEP 2. Drive your angst-ridden tween or teen to a nearby playground after the twelve-and-under crowd has left for their cocktail hour of bath, bed, and beyond.

STEP 3. Make everyone leave their phones in the car and get out. They'll look at you like you've lost your God-blessed mind, and you can expect a variety of grunts and huffing sounds as if air is leaking from their lungs and they're dying. Do not be alarmed, ignore all background noise, and quickly proceed to step 4.

STEP 4. Jauntily whistle your way over to a swing, without explanation. Do not speak. Talking to them is a trap! Although they are unable to turn off a light switch or replace the toilet

paper, they are MASTERS of debate … don't do it! Stay focused and continue playing your own game.

Just keep swinging … just keep swinging … just keep swinging.

STEP 5. Now, simply wait for it. If you stay strong and stick to the plan, eventually your play-deprived almost-adults won't be able to resist jumping in, or on, or down, as well. I promise. Give it a minute.

What your teens will never tell you is that sometimes they wish they were still able to run toward an open swing with wild abandon, or monkey around on the jungle gym like they used to when they were little. They miss the playground too. Don't let their Instagram feed fool you.

Stop Working Out

If you're one of these humans who eagerly anticipates your time at the gym, getting all giddy at the thought of treadmills and kettlebells and burpees, then just skip right on past this section. I'm not talking to you. Enjoy your stationary bike to nowhere. Have yourself a sweaty ball.

But if, like me, you suffer from WADD, or Workout Attention Deficit Disorder, you're my people.

I should preface this by saying that I am fully aware of the bountiful health and wellness benefits of a consistent fitness routine and regular exercise. We are a sedentary society, and we all need to get up from behind our screens a little more often and move it, move it. I understand that exercise makes us all faster, stronger, and more energized. I totally get it.

The problem is I don't find working out enjoyable. Like, at all. For the past year and a half I have been on a mission to find ways to turn my workout into a PLAYout. 'Cause I like to play . . . duh.

If you aren't happy about the way you choose to get fit and healthy . . . CHANGE IT NOW!

It doesn't have to be such a medicine-ball buster. Life is way too short to do stuff we loathe. And we all know we're more likely to keep doing stuff we actually enjoy.

Use the Personal Play Profile you completed at the start of this section (you did that, right?), and let it guide you. The way you loved to physically play as a youngster is probably how you'll love to physically play now.

Want to hate working out just a little less? Get fit like you did when you were five or fifteen.

* GO BACK TO DANCE CLASS. I meant to be a professional dancer when I grew up. As a young girl I took dance lessons at Sharon's School of Dance and was sure I had a future at American Ballet Theatre or, even better, an MTV music video. I'm still waiting for my call from Justin Timberlake or ABT. In the meantime, I've tried honing my skills at tap and ballet classes in my 'hood. I will say that donning pink tights and a black bodysuit after thirty years took some very deep breaths and a few *namastes*, but everyone's in the same ballet boat. And after the first few pliés, I had more fun doing cardio and toning my thighs than I had in years. Leaping and twirling never gets old. If you loved to dance as a kid . . . you'll love to dance now.

* **HOOPS FOR HEALTH:** So it turns out that hula hoops are the new dumbbell. Classes like "health hula" are popping up everywhere, and equipment like weighted hoops and "cardio core" fitness hoops, so you can shimmy your way to abs of steel, are not hard to find. Check out Hoopnotica.com. Prepare to be amazed.

* **THE PLAYGROUND CIRCUIT:** All that funky and free equipment hanging out at the playground is longing for you and your Lulus to jump aboard. Monkey bar pull-ups, park bench push-ups and triceps dips, sliding board sit-ups, sandbox lunges, and on and on and on. Wear those yoga pants to the playground, and actually work out in them!

* **WATER SPORTS:** Any class that involves a swimming pool, kickboards, pool noodles, and fins. #Winning

* **AERIAL YOGA:** If you haven't tried this, you must. Strapping yourself into a sling-like harness, hanging from the ceiling, and proceeding to do yoga poses in the air? Yes, please.

* **ROCK-CLIMBING CLASS:** Scaling a fake mountain with a harness around your arse is more fun than it sounds.

* **SKATING:** In-line skating, ice-skating, roller-skating!

* **BOXING CLASS:** I can't bear to watch the sport, but I do like to throw a good uppercut.

Find what floats your fitness boat, and go with that. Your goal here is to inject your regular workout routine with a healthy shot of playfulness so that you don't want to throw in the towel at the thought of exercising. You can do that, right?

Sitting Is the New Smoking

The average American spends approximately thirteen hours a day on his or her tokus. Research on "sitting disease" (seriously, that's an actual thing now) is showing a strong link between the sedentary lifestyle we lead and things like early-onset diabetes, cardiovascular disease, and even some cancers. Good grief.

Just fifteen minutes of mindful playtime is all it takes to jump-start your day. Whether you're a work-at-home parent, you have a job packed with meeting upon meeting, or you're stuck behind a computer for hours on end, taking short "play breaks" throughout your day will stimulate your creativity, productivity, and focus, while keeping your muscles from atrophying right before your very screen. When you hit that midday slump and all you want to do is suck down some caffeine or find a sleeping bag, take a break, STAND UP, and shake your sillies out.

Remember: This isn't about the kind of play you might be doing ALL DAY LONG with your little minions if you have 'em. This is playtime with the sole purpose of getting YOU fired up. If you have super-little kids, and the gift of fifteen to twenty minutes to yourself means one of two things—a power nap or a shower—then yeah, go. Sleep or clean thyself. Then come back to this list and grant yourself a play break at some point in your day. It'll make you feel as good as you do after a nap. Almost.

Keep a batch of these under your desk, in a pretty bin in the corner of your kitchen, or in your suitcase for work trips:

* A ukulele . . . you can learn to play some simple tunes online, regardless of your musical ineptitude
* A yoga ball
* A balance board

* A stack of origami paper and a good instruction book . . . start with the crane!
* A yo-yo
* Juggling balls
* Your dog's leash and a ball or Frisbee
* A playlist of five pop songs you're embarrassed you love, your iPhone, and a dance-worthy patch of floor
* A grown-up kick scooter . . . oh my gosh, so much more fun than you remember
* Small, desk-size versions of some games you loved as a kid, like Simon, Boggle, Connect Four (find an office mate who looks disgruntled and in need of play)

Pro tip: Consider setting your watch or phone alarm to go off a couple of times a day to signal that it's time to get up and shake it off.

Disclaimer: Your friends and neighbors may look at you funny and talk behind your back. And if they do, you're doing it right.

Stop Helicopter Parenting Yourself

When I taught preschool, one of my curriculum goals was helping children learn to take risks. Not dangerous, out-of-control risks, but thoughtful, courageous, and smart risks. Risks that would enable them to experience something brand-new and thrilling, or help them reach a self-motivated goal. It took time, encouragement, patience, and practice before most children learned to really trust their own abilities, limits, and risk-taking intuition. Risk-taking gets a bad rap. Those two words sound innately dangerous and scary, don't they?

Add to the effect that we reside in the era of the helicopter parent, over-the-top tiger moms, butterfly moms, and the ever-popular "free-range parenting" movement, some grown-ups aren't just afraid of letting their offspring take risks of any kind; they start drinking their own fear-flavored Kool-Aid and become equally resistant to taking risks of their own as well. Over the last several years, my desire to become more playful in my everyday life has meant having to teach myself the valuable and life-changing lesson of smart risk-taking, just as I tried to teach it to the three-, four-, and five-year-olds in my early childhood classroom.

When my husband, Jon, and I were nearing forty, we met a dynamic girl named Krista Parry, who was at the time the head of marketing for a very popular ski resort in Park City, Utah. Jon and I were both speaking at a social media conference there during the summer season, and upon meeting Krista, we were immediately drawn to her adventurous and playful spirit. Krista was there to promote her ski resort and the new program she had developed to help families discover and enjoy the sport of skiing together.

Throughout our conversations with Krista, she kept assuring my very skeptical husband that even though he was a long and lanky six-foot-seven, with size-16 feet, and we were both nearing middle age and had never skied before, we could and should learn to ski. As Krista exuberantly described how magnificent skiing would be for our whole family, Jon and I listened politely and nodded our heads. But later, all we could do was talk about how we couldn't imagine ever attempting to learn to ski this late in the game. Still, every time we bumped into Krista, she started up again, urging us to give it a go, encouraging words flying out of her big, perky smile.

She cautioned us that our young agile boys would be better skiers than us from the start, and that they would eventually turn into our instructors on the slopes, helping us face our fears and figure it all out. She described how we would connect and grow with them through the act of learning a new skill together. Having two boys nearing their teenage days who were becoming less and less interested in playing along with us, it was this notion of connecting with them in a fun new way that ultimately hooked us and convinced us to give skiing a try.

Krista invited us back for the upcoming ski season and said she would make sure we had stellar instruction. Which she did.

Lining up in the "Never Ever" lane at skiing lessons felt like being the new kid at a school in France when you only speak English, and have no idea what's going on around you, but everyone is super welcoming and the place is beyond beautiful. Equal parts terrifying and spectacular.

Jon and I silently side-eyed each other as we glided cautiously down the slight incline to the lift and shared the same thought that as scary and risky as this was going to be, we were about to experience something utterly fantastic.

Fast-forward five years, and downhill skiing has become my husband's absolute passion and very favorite way to play. Learning to ski at age forty was not pretty or effortless, make no mistake. And I'd like to take this opportunity to personally apologize to the seven children Jon leveled coming down the bunny hill for the first time. Sorry, guys, but he did holler "incoming!" as loud as he could.

Slowly yet surely, everything Krista Parry told us would happen has happened: the adrenaline-fueled family bonding created by learning something risky together, the heart-racing thrill of conquering a mountain we thought was wholly unattainable, the beauty of being vulnerable and brave in front of our kids, and the extreme joy of zipping down the slopes together, and talking excitedly during après-ski about how far we each had come. My sons are indeed the most patient and encouraging teachers when I don't know how to tackle a run or I'm scared to the point of tears at a risky first turn down a challenging slope. I once wailed, "I hate you allll" as I came flying down a terrifying first turn they forced me to try. And then we laughed until we wept.

And although Jon and I were initially motivated to learn to ski because of a desire to connect with our kids, learning to do something we thought we could not do revealed how much playful joy there is to be found when you decide to jump off a cliff (with a helmet and good instruction), and learn to fly on the way down. We ski WITH our boys, but honestly we ski FOR ourselves now. While they were definitely the main motivation for Jon and me to take on this new adventurous skill at mid-age, Jon especially has discovered something that truly makes his heart sing. A long, freshly powdered slope has become one of his most happy places to play.

Inviting more playfulness into your life might involve a dollop of risky business. Find something that thrills and slightly alarms you all at once, turn off the helicopter blades, and go for it.

Well Played

Laura Harrison Mayes, cofounder of the Mom 2.0 Summit

1. YOU NEED A FUNCTIONING BRAIN. Your brain is your BFF, and it needs a break. You should give it one. Because giving your top-notch brain the opportunity to get away and relax for a bit is the least you can do, really. You need to chill. That's just biology.

2. YOU THINK DIFFERENTLY IN A DIFFERENT PLACE. Perspective, new angles, creative ideas—all these things come from physically putting yourself in a different space. You never know what looking out on a new view can do for your outlook.

3. YOU AREN'T DEAD. Life is short, and there's a lot to see. Too often, we live heads-down in the tasks and the tedium. And while these weeds are inescapable elements that make up our days, they don't have to be our whole lives. (As Annie Dillard said, "How we spend our days is, of course, how we spend our lives.") And I want to spend my life alive.

4. YOUR TEN-YEAR-OLD SELF WILL HIGH-FIVE YOU. Remember when you wanted to be an adult because you could chew gum whenever you wanted? Well that's the part of you that could see how rad being a grown-up could be. The part of you that couldn't wait to go to a movie by yourself or eat ice cream for breakfast or buy a plane ticket to the Grand Canyon. You are now that adult. Don't let that ten-year-old down.

5. YOU DESERVE IT. You deserve to think creatively, to see things differently, to make connections with new perspectives and new people. Also, you totally can. Even with only a few dollars, even just a few miles away. I've seen first-hand how new ideas, new businesses and new friendships are formed through people playfully coming together to learn and grow. You should go for it. You deserve it. Your ten-year-old self would not disagree.

Incoming! Throw a Few "Play-Grenades" into Your Well-Planned Week.

Is your day-to-day beginning to feel like a playlist set on repeat?

Use your personal play profile to help you design a more playful life by tossing in some things that used to engulf your soul with flaming frivolity as a kid, or a few fun activities and games you've grown to adore as a grown-up. Doing just one thing a day that makes you feel more playful and less predictable will have a ripple effect, washing its happy juice over everything and everyone around you.

 Play-grenades are small, perspective-shifting fun bombs you can launch into your way-too-regular routine. With practice, you'll begin to recognize ways to lure your daily grind out of its broken record, playless existence. My personal favorite is "impromptu karaoke hour." We bought an inexpensive portable karaoke unit one New Year's Eve for our lake cottage, and I bust that baby out as often as possible.

Here are a few play-grenades to consider launching into your life when you've made some time for your own self.

Remember, playing for your SELF doesn't mean you have to wait until you're all alone. If you're habitually saving your personal play-time for when no one is around or bugging you, I'll see ya when your kids go to college. Stick some carpe into your diem, 'cause that diem of yours ain't getting any younger.

* Light some yummy candles, get into your "don't touch me" jammies (the baggy, comfy ones you wear when you want your spouse to know the kitchen is closed), take off your bra if applicable, grab a deck of cards, and play a game of solitaire.

* Pick one of the DIY projects you've pinned on Pinterest, then reserve yourself a Saturday morning and just finally DO IT.

* Catch fireflies after your kids go to bed.

* Instigate a pillow fight with your husband before bedtime.

* Get a battery-operated bubble machine from the toy aisle, put it on your kitchen island, and turn it on during the "witching hours," before or after dinner on a random Wednesday night.

* Rent a convertible for a half day, throw a scarf around your neck, and drive like it's 1959.

* Go skinny-dipping whenever PRIVATELY possible. I've gotten myself in a couple of awkward situations with this one. Still totally worth it.

* Send a long-distance friend a handmade, self-decorated card, and snail-mail it.

* Learn to whistle with your two fingers in your mouth. I'm still working on this one.

* Take a bubble bath and add way more bubbles than you should.

* Blow bubbles with bubble gum (Bubble Yum grape flavor is the best), get really good at it, and challenge your kids or your partner to a bubble-off.

* Honestly, do anything involving bubbles.

* Get yourself a pair of roller skates (and all the safety padding), and pretend it's 1982 in your driveway.

* Nab yourself a small personal trampoline, put it in front of the TV, and watch Bravo while you bounce.

SPRAY PAINT STATEMENTS

What You'll Need

* A piece of old jewelry (I recommend visiting your local thrift shop to find something fun and bold that's looking for a second life.)
* White nontoxic spray paint
* Nontoxic spray paint in the color of your choice

Directions

1. Rip a few pages of inspiration out of your favorite magazine to protect your surface from the spray paint.

....

2. Lay the necklace or bracelet on top of the magazine pages.

....

3. Spray your piece of jewelry with the white spray paint. This may take a few coats to get everything covered in white, but make sure to let each coat dry before applying another.

....

4. When your jewelry is completely white and the paint has dried, you're ready to add some color! This may also take a few coats to get it just the right shade.

....

5. Let your jewelry dry overnight, then wear your new statement piece on date night!

Tips on how to choose a color for your necklace:

* Choose your favorite color to accessorize with.
* Go bright and bold! Choose a neon for a true playful POP of color!

Push Re-PLAY

Think of a re-PLAY as a way to revisit and reconstruct some of the playful activities you absolutely LOVED as a child, restyling them for your adult life. The personal play profile you completed at the start of this section will again aid you with this. You did complete that play profile, didn't you?

Go back and take a look at some of the things you mentioned there. Very often, the experiences and activities we adored most as youngsters will bring us the same level of delight as grown-ups. We might not be able to reproduce them exactly, but we can reinvent them and "re-PLAY" them all over again. Here are a few examples to get your own ball rolling:

5 Instant Re-PLAYS

1. YOU ADORED ROLLING, SMASHING, AND CREATING WITH CLAY AND DOUGH AS A KID. Re-PLAY that creative joy by signing up for a weekend pottery class in your community. I took a throwing class back in my twenties, and the act of getting my hands and the rest of me muddy as I delicately tried to shape and mold that clay somersaulted me back to my tomboy days of making mud pies with my brothers on the hill behind our apartment building, and my strong admiration for Play-Doh. Go get dirty all by yourself. You only have to clean up you!

2. YOU SPENT HOURS AS A TEENAGER RIPPING APART FASHION MAGS AND PIECING THE SCRAPS TOGETHER INTO EPIC COLLAGES. Re-PLAY that artistic fun using your favorite periodicals and the inside of a cupboard or closet door, or a

white foam-core board to create an inspiration mash-up of the looks, recipes, or style ideas you want to try. It's JUST as much fun as it was when you were fifteen!

3. YOU AND YOUR BOX OF SIXTY-FOUR CRAYOLA CRAYONS WERE BESTIES, AND YOU SO TOTALLY SHOULD HAVE WON THE COLORING CONTEST AT THE MALL. Good news! Adult coloring books are the new black. Check your local bookstore or online retailer for coloring books full of beautiful botanicals, intricate mandalas, or complex geographic designs. There is Zen enlightenment in a well-colored page. I even have a friend who was prescribed coloring sessions to combat her seasonal depression. Truth.

4. YOU WERE THE FEMALE EQUIVALENT OF HANDYMAN NEGRI FROM *MISTER ROGERS' NEIGHBORHOOD*. Constructing, creating, and building never grows old, even when we do. One of my favorite places to buy cool building sets is Marbles the Brain Store. They have all sorts of games, toys, and construction sets for both the young and the simply young at heart. I like to keep a pretty bowl of smooth wooden old-school blocks or Jenga blocks right on my coffee table or kitchen island (if you do it right, it looks like a modern art piece), so that this brain-boosting fruit is always ripe for the pickin' and playin'.

5. YOU WERE A LITTLE MONET. Pick up a basic watercolor kit, set up a small easel, and grab some brushes! There are inexpensive, portable tabletop easels you can pop on your kitchen island or take to a playground or park. I have less than zero fine arts skills, and that's okay because no one's going to buy my masterpiece anyway. There is brilliance anytime a brush full of vibrant color is swept across a vacant white backdrop. No personal or professional judgment allowed here. The journey is the destination, folks.

YOU'VE GOT MAIL

What You'll Need

* Super fun stationery: Look for some in a paper store, or pick up some wonky misfit cards from a thrift shop.
* Stamps: Check out USPS.com to find some more fun collections that might not be available in your local post office.
* Optional: Colorful pens, confetti, stickers

Directions

Everybody loves mail . . . when it isn't a bill or an advertisement. Why not send your pals a lil' something special snail-mail style? First step: Put on your fave show to binge watch and get all your materials set in front of you. Keep it simple with an inside joke inside your card, or write a heartfelt message to your friend. Sprinkle a little confetti in the envelope, stick on a stamp, and send it off.

Tip: For a romantic spin, send a letter in the mail to your partner with a special message. It's something they won't be expecting at all and will totally brighten their day.

The Art of PLAY-gerism

Copy from Your Kids

My boys have introduced me to things I simply would never have tried had I not had them. I grew up with two older brothers and have always been willing to try almost anything once, but these boys have upped the brave-and-daring ante. Girls are just as daring and brave and fun as boys, but I have boys so that's my POV. #girlpower

Recently my son Maxwell begged me to jump on these Razor dirt bikes I had gotten to test out for a TV segment. The boys LOVED them and wanted me to experience the thrill of zipping down the dirt road behind our lake cottage. When he first asked I said "uh, NO" without even thinking about it. They scared me a little, and at fortysomething, skinned knees just aren't sexy.

After fifteen minutes of Max's ~~badgering~~ encouraging, I realized I can't really spend my time writing about being playfully brave and then totally wimp out and never try. I hopped on my own little dirt bike, got a quick tutorial from Maxwell on braking and turning, and we were off.

Sweet mother-of-pearl. Dirt bikes are a flipping BLAST! Who knew?

Our kids knew. That's who.

The biggest lesson I learned that morning was that you must take a deliberate pause before saying no to your kids' crazy requests for play. And then ask yourself "Why am I saying no?" If you're saying no to something a little risky because you really do not feel it's something you can or want to do, then no it is.

But if you're saying no because it makes you a little nervous, or you're afraid to look foolish, or you think you won't be able to do it well, then consider doing it anyway.

The look on Maxwell's face as I zipped past him on my dirt bike, ponytail flapping in the wind, grinning from ear to ear, was worth a million dollars. But what it did to my own playful spirit was priceless.

It's a really good idea to copy your children's risky and radical behavior. Most of the time.

Beat Your Kids' High Score

Not all video games are the devil's spawn. I will confess that as a teacher with a master's degree in education, I've been a bit bigoted when it comes to the playing of video games, and screen time in general. I spent many, many years considering video games the Darth Vader of creative play. I complained about them often, I used them as currency with my kids to be quickly taken away for bad behavior, and I lumped them all into the play palace of evil.

I would constantly tell my boys that they needed more REAL play, hands-on discovering, and physical activities—and less digital playtime. And I still believe that. But after spending the last seven years working with major toy companies, including the video game ones, for my website, magazine column, and TV segments, I've realized that not all digi-play is created equal. There are some amazingly fun, highly entertaining, and dare I say quite educational video games on the market today. Once I stopped being the nagging naysayer all the time and actually played some of these games with my kids, I realized why they like them so

much. Recently I've started playing some of them when my kids aren't even around. Shh . . .

Need a twenty-minute pop of playfulness? Try one of these.

(Don't tell your kids you've gotten really good, and when they ask you to play with them next time, give them a very disinterested "Well, um, hmmmm, allll right," in your best martyr-mom voice. Then crush them.)

10 Video Games You'll Love Playing WithOUT Your Kids

1. Disney Infinity
2. Mario Kart
3. SingStar
4. Wii Sports. Tennis is my favorite!
5. Minecraft for XBox 360 (seriously)
6. The Sims
7. Just Dance
8. Mario Party: Island Tour
9. Wipeout
10. LEGO Series: Harry Potter, Batman, Star Wars

Copy Your Friends

If you're still having trouble incorporating personal play breaks through-out your work week, and you just don't think you have the time, I suggest taking a cue from your most playful friends. We all have them, or should.

I happen to have several pals who inspire me daily to include myself on my never-ending list of things to do for all the people in my life. My friend Annie, for example, LOVES her bike. I mean L.O.V.E. in deep red lipstick kind of love. I don't think I've ever known anyone who enjoys a solo bike ride more than Annie. I remember when she first started taking her long treks down the bike path from our North Shore suburb into the city of Chicago, and I jealously wondered how in heaven's name she had the time! She's a mom of three active kids, has authored two books, runs a household, and has just as much on her plate as everyone else. Yet Annie frequently MAKES time for this playful activity that brings her great joy. She intentionally made space so that when her playful spirit came a-knockin' and the day was ripe for the pickin', she was able to go, go, go.

Annie's love for her bicycle has inspired me to get my own two-wheeler down from the rack in my garage, buy a cute basket for the front, and rediscover the joy of the ride. It's now become one of my favorite playful escapes as well. I don't go all the way to the city for half the day, but simply tooling around my 'hood for a half hour makes me feel ten again. Now all I need is a banana seat, some plastic handlebar streamers, and a bell, and it's 1979 all over again.

Then there are my pals Sari and Kimbra. These girls, like Annie, are two of my spur-of-the-moment playmakers. Sari and Kimbra are the pals who send me all-of-a-sudden text messages like "Wanna go paddleboarding?!" or "Meet me at the beach?" or "Come over to my backyard for an hour before the kids get home from school!"

And even though I can't always run away with them when they send out the Bat-Signal of playful bliss, these friends are a beautiful reminder to me of why it's good to leave space for the spontaneous. I work from home and have a more flexible schedule than most. But I often fill it to the brim, allowing no wiggle room whatsoever. Not conducive to a well-played life at all.

Obviously, most folks aren't able to simply run away from work in the middle of the day when their playful spirit starts poking them, either. The key here is allowing for the possibility that a playful moment might

show up, and intentionally leaving just a little crack in the door of your day, so it can come on in if it does.

My husband does this really well. His weekends are a sacred space on our family calendar. He cherishes those two days of reconnecting with himself and his family, and is quite protective of those forty-eight hours of frivolity that happen only four times a month. As a television producer, his days are jammed with a multitude of meetings and shoots and putting out TV-making fires while trying to create something entertaining. His is the kind of job that requires availability pretty much 24/7. I've learned to be unoffended when dinners and dates and evening plans are abruptly interrupted because production on a show has just imploded or a celeb is having a meltdown. It's par for the course.

A lot of you, no matter what your profession, can relate to this hamster wheel of work, work, work. I know. Americans work a whole heck of a lot.

So when the weekend rolls in, and Jon isn't on a shoot, he takes playtime with his family very seriously.

He tries with all his might to hold impenetrable space for what fills him up most fully: his family and closest friends. I admire how Jon easily says "no thank you" to things that don't meet his need to refuel. He feels absolutely zero fear of missing out, nor obligatory guilt. He does not say "yes" when everything in him is yelling "no, no, no!"

Of course there are times we do not-so-playful things for others on the weekends to be helpful or supportive. There is also great benefit in serving others when you (seemingly) get nothing in return. But what I've learned over the last twenty-five years of being married to Jon is the importance of holding fast to the stuff that replenishes our fun-tanks. For Jon, those things are:

* Our unplugged lake cottage in the woods
* His Triumph motorcycle

* Goofing around in the backyard with our boys
* Skiing
* Riding his road bike
* Walking to Hartigan's, our local ice cream shop, for waffle cones
* Jumping into Lake Michigan from an anchored WaveRunner
* Table shuffleboard tournaments in the basement
* Being fully open to the spontaneous fun that just might show up at his door

I admire how Jon does not merely talk the talk, he also walks the walk.

If you need inspiration to play for yourself, take a closer look at how your well-played friends and family are tapping into their own playful sides, and copycat the hell out of them.

Use the blank list below to jot down ten ways you would love to get your play ON, for the benefit of your own playful spirit, over the next couple of months. Make sure to include simple, no-cost, quickie activities and ideas, along with a few more elaborate playdates for one. This is NOT another to-do list! No one will be grading or judging or checking to make sure you complete the items on your wish list. Aim to fit just one thing from your playlist into your busy life each weekend. Remember, this list is between you and your inner eight-year-old. Go ask her what she wants to do! She's very excited right now.

How I Long to PLAY All by Myself

1. _____
2. _____
3. _____
4. _____
5. _____
6. _____
7. _____
8. _____
9. _____
10. _____

Learn Yourself a New Trick

I'm talking party tricks here, y'all. Quirky weird stuff that you pull out at stuffy cocktail parties and when you want to slightly embarrass your kids and fully impress your friends all at once. Do you have a signature party trick? Maybe it's time to get yourself one.

Anytime we twist our brains in a creative and playful new way, we stimulate the frontal cortex and help boost our memory, focus, and mental flexibility. So basically, learning how to pull a golf ball out of your mouth could get you into Mensa. Don't quote me on that, okay? Plus, more people will invite you to their parties. So there's that.

5 Playful Party Tricks to Start Practicing Right Now

1. The cherry stem tongue-tying trick
2. Juggling lemons or limes

3. The coin coming out of someone's ear trick
4. How to rub your tummy and pat your head at the same time
5. A fabulous card trick no one's ever seen before. YouTube is a great place to learn these!

Party of One

How often are you all alone? I'm talkin' straight-up all by yourself, with no one to talk to but the dog, alone?

If you have a job and small children and a partner and a bunch of friends, then the answer is most likely never ever.

Historically I would describe myself as someone who doesn't really enjoy being alone. When things become too quiet or solitary for too long, I get suspicious and slightly nervous and a little creeped out, and then I usually begin singing to myself just to fill the dead air, which makes it even creepier, and the whole cycle starts again. Adorable, no?

However, thanks to our culture's obsession with labeling one another, and the help of BuzzFeed quizzes and listicles helping us figure out if we're extroverted, introverted, intro-extroverted, extro-introverted, or just plain weird, I've discovered that to function most fully, I need extended periods of playful privacy—aka alone time. Turns out that most people do, too.

Even the most extro of the extroverts could use some time by themselves, left solely to their own vices and devices. For us extroverts, allowing for and getting comfy within our own four walls takes practice. I have some very close friends who are introverts and fully embrace the beauty of playing alone. I discovered that by watching and learning from these masters of solitary refinement.

It's in this space that deeply good things occur. When we gift ourselves with wide-open spaces in which to wonder and daydream and

fiddle and play all by ourselves, we tap into a magical place of renewal and connection with our own creative souls.

If you do have time alone, how do you most often spend it? Looking at other people's playfulness and good times on one social platform or another?

Disconnect for even an hour or two a week to dance to your own music.

Play Maker 11 PLAYFUL TUNES TO GET YOUR PERSONAL PARTY STARTED

Joe Saylor (aka Tambourine Cowboy), of Jon Batiste and Stay Human, house band of *The Late Show with Stephen Colbert*

1. "Simple Things"—Minnie Riperton
2. "Love Machine"—The Miracles
3. "Don't Talk About Me"—Tony! Toni! Toné!
4. "Believe"—Jon Batiste and Stay Human
5. "Sugar Foot Stomp"—Fletcher Henderson
6. "I Want You Back"—The Jackson 5
7. "Handa Wanda"—Bo Dollis
8. "Love Train"—The O'Jays
9. "Rhythm of the Night"—DeBarge
10. "Breezin'"—George Benson
11. "Java"—Allen Toussaint

A Few Things to Do While Leaving Yourself All Alone

* Grab a big blanket, head outside, look up at the sky, and play the "what crazy stuff do you see in the clouds?" game.
* Take a horseback riding lesson.
* Rent a kayak, canoe, or paddleboard . . . all of these are easy to do!

* Walk through the woods, stopping to collect natural treasures.
* Climb a tree. Don't skip this one. Pick a tree and climb it.
* Skip rope . . . not to lose weight, just to skip and jump.
* Bake cupcakes—and not for a bake sale.
* Explore your way down a local trail, beside a creek, or anywhere that's green.
* Collect wildflowers and press them into a heavy book.
* Make snow angels.
* Collect fall leaves and iron them between wax paper.
* Learn to identify four constellations in the night sky, and then show your kids.
* Play Scrabble against yourself . . . yes, literally play both sides of the board.
* Reread your favorite book from when you were a teenager.
* Learn to can pickles or peaches, and you'll feel like Laura Ingalls Wilder.

Hide a Secret Stash

If you aren't hiding stashes of your favorite things from your kids, you haven't truly earned your parent card. It's a rite of passage. Kids can be judgy. It might be your favorite dark chocolate or some junk food (cough, cough, Skittles, cough) that you've told them is the devil's handiwork, or your subscription to *US Weekly*, or the Prosecco you unearth each week while watching *Real Housewives of New York City*. Sometimes secrets are a super good thing.

Compile a toy box of sorts filled with fun and frivolity that you can pull out when the going gets tough and you need a quirky quickie.

I made one of these recently for my girlfriend Sari in celebration of her birthday, and she was over the moon. I called it her Play Crate for One. It's easy to assemble, doesn't have to be pricey, and will be a lifesaver in a much-needed moment.

Pick up a photo storage box, a happy container from The Container Store, or if you're feeling very artsy/craftsy, decorate a shoe box! Next, fill it with small playthings that will help to snap you out of that cranky mood or stressful situation. Keep it in the glove compartment of your car, under your bed, in a drawer in the kitchen, or up on a shelf your kids can't reach.

Of course you can share your playthings with your younguns if you have 'em, but I wouldn't.

This play crate should be designed with you in mind. Stock it with things that will encourage you to stop being so grown up for a minute.

Have fun with this. It's not meant to be rocket physics. Your local party store or craft store is a great place to hunt and gather your goods.

Here are some things you might want to include:

* A glow-in-the-dark yo-yo
* A kazoo

- A can of Silly String
- A mini bottle of bubbles
- A set of shiny jacks
- A small sketch pad and pretty colored pencils
- A whoopee cushion

- A mini Slinky
- A pair of goofy sunglasses or Groucho Marx specs
- A key-chain-size Nerf Dart Blaster (these exist, and they're fabulous)
- A small watercolor set
- Silly Putty

- Mini washi tape spools in playful colors
- Temporary tattoos (the jewelry ones rule!)
- A mini Etch A Sketch
- Any little thing that sparks open-ended playfulness in your overscheduled life

Wander Aimlessly

Are you a curious, independent wanderer or a Nervous Nelly scared to explore alone?

For most of my adult life I was the latter. I rarely, if ever went off exploring new places all by myself. Wandering around a new neighborhood, city, or museum wasn't my jam and would never be my notion of fun. I just didn't see the point of wandering if I didn't have someone with whom to wander. And I honestly didn't "get" the people who did.

When we moved to Chicago, for example, we were given a temporary apartment right off Michigan Avenue. I spent a whole month right in the heart of that fabulous city footloose and fancy-free, with no kids or a

job, rarely venturing too far from our high-rise abode for fear of getting lost, or mugged, in broad daylight. It's on my list of regrets.

I now cringe when I think about it. What I would GIVE to have a rent-free apartment in the heart of Chicago and weeks to myself. Oh, the places I'd go!

It just took watching more-fearless friends of mine who were so comfortable heading into an unfamiliar neighborhood or town or wooded path and simply being open to what they might find. I wanted to be like them—comfortable enough to curiously wander and explore. My brother Sean is one of those happy wanderers. Before he was married, he would routinely fly off to new cities or foreign lands all by himself and figure it out when he got there. It was actually one of his favorite things to do. I have girlfriends who do the same thing on a smaller scale, driving to new neighborhoods and seeing what they find. I've always wanted to be less afraid and more daring that way.

I finally understand and am getting comfortable with what my wandering friends and family already knew was wonderful. That there is a thrilling kind of butterflies-in-the-stomach thing that happens when you wander for the sake of wandering, wide open to the playfulness that is intrinsic in the unexpected. And that the cliché quote "Not all who wander are lost"—or get lost—happens to be true. Once you try it, it becomes slightly addictive.

I'm slowly getting better at being a good wanderer.

Some of the Best Places to Wander Aimlessly

* A forest preserve or nature path

* A neighborhood that's not your own

* A nearby town that your friends are always raving about

* An unfamiliar bookstore

* The farmers' market

* A batch of art galleries (plan to hit several in one outing)

* Vintage and secondhand stores

* A part of your own city you've never explored

* A nearby college campus

* Manhattan. I go often for work, you're never really alone, and it never gets old.

* Over the river and through the woods

List three places you'd be open to wandering playfully:

Where I Would LOVE to Wander Aimlessly

1.

2.

3.

Consume Playful Media

We are what we consume. You've heard the phrases "you are what you eat" and "garbage in, garbage out," right?

Yeah, well, that goes for what we eat, but it also goes for what we watch, listen to, play with, and read. You want to be fearful and anxious? Watch horror movies and read scary novels. You want to feel depressed and alarmed? Watch the evening news. You want to be happy, playful, and positive? Consume happy, playful, and positive media.

We can't always live in the land of Oz and only consume the happy, playful stuff, I know, I know. A girl can dream.

But we can choose to pop more playful and uplifting media into our every day. So when you need a little levity and laughter, I've got your back. Spend more time in the positive and playful and you'll be more positive and playful. It's science. I'm pretty sure.

Watch Playful Stuff

Most of us have only a few hours a day to sit back and watch something for fun. Maybe you have thirty minutes on your lunch break with which to watch a TED Talk, or a batch of YouTube videos, and perhaps a couple of viewing hours after the kids go to bed and before your eyes begin to glaze over. What do you generally choose to watch when no one's looking?

I'm someone who holds on tightly to the media I consume. I can't watch scary stuff or violent stuff, even if it's make-believe, because it sticks like glue to my brain long after I click or switch away. The evening news is tough for me. I get most of my worldly information from my daily e-mails from the sarcastically clever girls over at The Skimm, and I'm totally okay with that. Whether you're a bit media-wimpy like me, or you don't seem to be bothered by intense television, movies, or online video content, I believe the choices we consistently make with the media we consume does effect our overall inner "vibe." I've seen it in the children I taught in the elementary classroom, and the kids in my own home.

I'm not saying that watching horror movies, violent TV shows, or a show full of bad news makes us psychotic, violent, and depressed. As adults we tend to understand what is pretend and what is for real, and we can take bad news and work through it.

But along with all of the grown-up serious stuff in our Internet feeds, television news channels, and Netflix queues, it's important to sprinkle some lighthearted, playful-spirit-boosting, happy media on top. Take inventory of the media you regularly consume, and see if you need a shot of something playful and positive.

Here's some of the playful stuff I'm digging these days:

15 Things I Think You'd Like to Watch

1. *Good Mythical Morning*
2. *Unbreakable Kimmy Schmidt*
3. *Comedians in Cars Getting Coffee*
4. Old-school musicals
5. *Pursuit of Sexiness*
6. *Notary Publix*

7. *Maria Bamford Show*
8. *Between Two Ferns*
9. *Catastrophe*
10. *Broad City*
11. *Inside Amy Schumer*
12. *Key and Peele*
13. *Smart Girls at the Party*
14. *Girls with Glasses*
15. *Friends*

Now it's your turn.

Conduct a "playful stuff to watch" hunt of your own! Ask your BFFs, your kids, your Facebook friends, your colorist, or anyone else you find particularly delightful, what they're watching that's sparking their playful side. Then use the following space to create your own list of merry media to pop into your alone time.

1. _____
2. _____
3. _____
4. _____
5. _____
6. _____
7. _____
8. _____
9. _____
10. _____

Listen to Playful Stuff

Podcasts are the new radio show, and there are literally loads of them out there banging around the interwebs. They're a great thing to click on during your lunch break, while washing dishes, doing carpool (before your kids get in the car), running errands, or relaxing before bedtime. There are many great family-friendly podcasts that your kids will love, but the audio shows below are ones I think you'll enjoy all for yourself.

15 Podcasts You Should Definitely Subscribe To

1. *The Dinner Party Download*
2. *Wait Wait . . . Don't Tell Me!*
3. *StarTalk* with Neil deGrasse Tyson
4. *The Nerdist*
5. *Kicking and Screaming*
6. *My Brother, My Brother and Me*
7. *Stuff You Should Know*
8. *The Moth*
9. *Comedy Bang! Bang!*
10. *Call Your Girlfriend*
11. *Pop Culture Happy Hour*
12. *Urban Coffee*
13. *Laugh or Go Crazy*
14. *How Did This Get Made?*
15. *The Right Reasons*

Read Playful Stuff

We don't read books like we used to. I mean real books with pages and chapters and good content. So big hugs to you for reading mine! Now here are some other playful and clever publications I think you need to stack on your nightstand.

15 Playfully Written Books That Will Make You LOL for REALZ

1. *Bossypants* by Tina Fey
2. *Good Omens* by Terry Pratchett and Neil Gaiman
3. *Mr. Bison's Journal* by Edward Bison
4. *Yes Please* by Amy Poehler
5. *Selp-Helf* by Miranda Sings
6. *Is Everyone Hanging Out Without Me?* by Mindy Kaling
7. *The Sweet Potato Queens' Book of Love* by Jill Conner Browne
8. *I Was Told There'd Be Cake* by Sloane Crosley
9. *I Love You More Than You Know* by Jonathan Ames
10. *I Remember Nothing* by Nora Ephron
11. *Why I Hate Straws* by Barry Parham
12. *Someone Could Get Hurt* by Drew Magary
13. *Modern Romance* by Aziz Ansari and Eric Klinenberg
14. *Me Talk Pretty One Day* by David Sedaris
15. *The Bedwetter: Stories of Courage, Redemption, and Pee* by Sarah Silverman

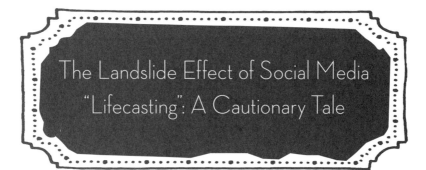

The Landslide Effect of Social Media "Lifecasting": A Cautionary Tale

Techopedia defines "lifecasting" as "uninterrupted streaming of an individual's daily life," adding that "lifecasters are seen as the polar opposite of privacy enthusiasts in that they willingly post every detail of their lives for the public to see."

When you think of lifecasters, think Kim Kardashian and those Instagrammers who think we really care what their kids had for lunch, if they are going to wear jeans or leggings, and how many times they blinked their eyes today. Social sharing is wonderful; lifecasting slays your playful spirit.

And makes people think you're a total narcissist. Which I know you're not. I have spent the last twelve years sharing my life and developing my brand in the social media space. I post something every day or two, on one platform or another, unless I'm on vacation or it's the weekend, and I shut it down to be unplugged and focus on my family.

I have definitely been tempted more than once to join the litany of lifecasters, since it seemed the thing to do to "build my brand" and keep people "engaged."

Thankfully, each time I started down that post-every-fricking-thing path, my family was firmly against it. They are a smart lot.

You see, for me, social sharing started with my little mom blog and

a small Twitter following way back in 2005. Over the years, I've played around with YouTube, became known as a "vlogger," joined the throng of Instagrammers (@meredithplays in case you want to follow along), built a bigger website, started doing more television appearances, and now have become an author. All in large part because I share my stuff on social media. I don't hate social media. On the contrary. This space has been very good to me.

But over the last decade, I've watched the social sharing landscape grow and change and develop into a happily overpopulated and desegregated pond where everyone, not just bloggers or online personalities, feels welcome to jump in and live their lives in front of a vast audience of likers, followers, lovers, and haters. It's amazing and wonderful in so many ways, isn't it?

But as lifecasting starts to become the modus operandi for many, it's also apparent that the quest for outside approval, mostly from people we'll never meet, becomes quite alluring to our needy, insatiable little egos and self-worth.

Social media is a city that never sleeps, with a population that is loyally there to feed our desire to be seen and heard and approved. At all times. A very fine double-edged sword, indeed.

No doubt, social media platforms provide us with the fabulous opportunity to share our ideas, experiences, and personal moments with long-lost friends, far-off family, and folks from all over the interworld, and no doubt, social media has certainly helped me and many others grow their brands and businesses. But like most things, it's the extreme measures that can ultimately do us in and can take us down. And conditions are getting increasingly extreme.

There's a living-for-everyone's-applause landslide that can occur when our social media sharing morphs into a distracted preoccupation with the prescribed and contrived story we are hoping to portray, for a far-off audience's approval.

So, what happens when we start living for the likes? I can tell you what happens because I have gotten just as sucked up in it as the rest of you who are playing a digital version of Marco Polo in the posting pond.

What happens is that we begin to relinquish the present moment and those within it, even if it's just ourselves, in return for a quick fix of validation and applause. We yell "Marco!" to our crowd of cyber friends and followers, and if no one yells "Polo!" back, we feel like we're doing something wrong.

Simply put, lifecasting leaves little room for fully authentic, joy-FULL, and purely playful experiences. Whether you're in a group or all by yourself, you simply cannot be present in two places at once. It's time to get back to the present moment a bit more and remember what it's like to play just for ourselves.

If you feel like you need help Snapchatting your way out of that NEED for the feed, I have a few tricks that have helped me disconnect and play-fully reconnect with myself and the very underrated present moment.

Here are three steps to breaking your oversharing addiction and re-discovering how much fun it is to play for yourself:

1. In the words of Mrs. Incredible: "DISENGAGE. I repeat, DIS-EN-GAGE!"

If a magical moment happens in the woods, or anywhere else, and no one is there to see it, share it, like it, and repost it . . . did it really happen?

For many folks, unfortunately, the answer is "nope." Social media platforms are a seductive siren that never stops singing. Never.

Over the last couple of years I have become just as intentional about disengaging as I have been about engaging on social platforms. And I've finally come to the conclusion that it's the folks you don't see 24/7 in the feed who are actually doing the best

stuff and probably having the most fun. I make time to play for myself by riding my bike, baking cupcakes, getting crafty, playing my uke, and then I intentionally DON'T post it on Instagram or Facebook. Imagine! I absolutely still post those things from time to time, but there's a little more personal pleasure in those things in the moments when I don't. Weird, but true. Try it and you'll see what I mean.

2 LOG THE HECK OUT. Social media is like heroin for extroverts. And I'm a major extrovert. As I've stated, I have been addicted to the feed, so I know of what I speak. I am a recovering Facebook-aholic and Instagram junkie, often unable to refrain from clicking in habitually throughout the day to see what all of my friends are doing at the party without me. It's been during the writing of this book, actually, that I've realized just how alluring and addictive the constant flow of everyone else's business can be.

If you too struggle with the continual check-in, try simply logging OUT. Logging out of Facebook, Instagram, or other social platforms cuts off the communal online chatter and puts me front and center with the project I need to complete, or the solo activity I want just for me, or the uninterrupted time I long to spend with my fam. This must sound a little twelve-step-programmy to all you introverted nonsharers. But if you know, you know. My only advice when logging out for a stretch: Write down your passwords before you leave the party.

3. Like your own damn self.

This step seems the simplest, and yet it's the most important and profound: Be your own most loyal and thumbs-up-giving follower!

Like your own damn self a little more often. For most folks, this takes frequent practice, especially in the new millennium where "likes" are our fastest-growing currency. Playing alone now and again, sharing a spirit-lifting, creative experience with only me, myself, and I, and being impressed with myself FIRST can be just as addictive as watching your Instagram photo rack up the hearts. And then when you see how awesome it is for you, make sure to share that awesome with your kids; most of them don't remember a time when having followers meant something creepy. Leading by example is a real thing.

Now it's your turn, oversharers! Use this blank list below to jot down five ways you want to play for yourself in the coming weeks, and not tell a single soul. You're going to totally dig it.

1. _____

2. _____

3. _____

4. _____

5. _____

A Permission Slip for PLAY

Hooray! We're almost home!

I'm so proud of you for getting your permission slip signed, packing your lunch, throwing on your adventure shoes, and jumping on the *Well Played* party bus with me! You deserve a cookie.

We're coming to the end of our fun-fueled field trip together and I hope you've thoroughly enjoyed the journey . . . or at the very least you didn't get lost, sunburned, or motion sick.

I also hope this book has been excitedly thrown aside many times, during spontaneous fits of frivolity-seeking and the overwhelming desire to skip, throw, run, bounce, paint, jump, dance, sing, color, create, and PLAY!

I hope you're all nodding with me now as I tell you one more time that play is the most unbound, ego-free expression of our truest selves; a big ridiculous cannonball right into your personal pool of happiness.

Unabashed playfulness hydrates our relationships with Super Soakers of connective goodness and present-moment joy.

Like prayer, mediation, therapy, yoga, a great run, or a healthy "roll in the hay," the practice of playfulness is game-changing and deeply beneficial to our overall well-being.

Even twenty minutes a day of intentional idiocracy, spontaneous creative combustion, or purposeful PLAYtime, has the power to make you even more amazing and delightful than you already are! I know that sounds impossible, 'cause you're already so darn amazing and delightful, but it can. I promise!

The only thing left to do now is grant yourself the permission to dive into that pond of playfulness as often as possible, and over and over and over again. Especially when you're just too "busy," you have very serious stuff to do, and life is all kinds of overwhelming. In the words of Dory: "Just keep swimming, just keep swimming."

I'll be on this crazy field trip with you every day as well. While I'm often the whistle-wearing chaperone, leading the charge, some days I'm also the kindergartener who needs the group to hold my hand, tie my shoes, and make sure I don't get lost in the shuffle.

But what I know for darn-tootin' sure is that it is indeed a happy talent to know how to play. And I'm way better at my craft when I practice a little bit every single day.

Now, let's get back on the bus!

Acknowledgments

To my literary agent, Fran Black, for championing this book, talking me off the ledge more than once, and being the best cheerleader ever. Thank you for your unshakable belief in me.

To Lisa Sharkey, for "getting" this book right away, and for putting your vision, brilliance, and talent behind it. You amaze me.

To my editor, Amy Bendell, for loving this book from the start, and always being so generous with your smart, positive, and productive guidance. Thank you for your confidence in me.

To my assistant editor, Alieza Schvimer, for your steady direction, enthusiasm, and kindness. It spurred me on to just keep writing . . . just keep writing . . . Thanks for being my go-to girl.

Acknowledgments

To my parents, for being my biggest fans and always clapping the loudest. I love you.

To June and John, for deeply loving me like one of your own.

To my big brothers, Sean and Daren, for teaching me how to throw a spiral, play in the dirt, and always keep up with the boys.

To the girls in the 'hood, Laurie Cavalier, Lauri Harris, Elizabeth Nasser, Beth Aldrich, Cheryl Leahy, Geraldine Lana, Doreen Rothstein, Pam Fowler, Kimberly Alcantara, Erin Lyons, Jill Sutherland, and Ann Scortino. I will deeply miss Mom Movie Nights and your fabulous friendship.

To Annie Burnside, for finding me on the kindergarten playground and for the last twelve years of inappropriate, deeply fun, and love-filled friendship.

To Kimbra Burnside, for being that friend who cares and loves the hardest. I am so grateful for it. You are one of a kind.

To Sari Shein, for your laugh, your loyalty, and your "hell yes" mentality. We'll always have Harlem.

To Suzanne Armstrong, for your creativity and friendship, and for being the best production assistant around.

To Jim Higley, for being one of the best listeners I've ever met, and for showing us all how to truly live our best lives. See ya in L.A.!

To Alaina Buzas, for being my "web girl" and creative helper on all things "Team Meredith." Here's to the next adventure!

To my 15701 playmates: Tina, Stephanie, Jenny, Lyndee, Morgan, and Missy. #IHSforever.

To my blogging community, I am so grateful for your ten years of friendship, support, fun, and understanding of the "hustle." You'll always be home base.

To Tamara O'Shaughnessy, for allowing me to write for your magazine, and for being the best editor a girl could ask for.

To Samantha Martin, for your belief, hard work, and helping me take my vision from a convo on the floor to all of THIS. You're a force.

To Caitlin Giles and Sara Fisher at 2 Moms Media, for your creative, smart, and stellar work on our *Well Played* events and beyond.

To Alicia Ybarbo, for giving me my first shot on national TV at the *Today* show. Thanks for believing I could do it.

To producer Sarah Clagett, for continuing to believe in what I have to share with your *Today* show audience. Honored to be a part of it.

To Anne Keenan Higgins, you made this book come to life. I feel so blessed to have you as my illustrator. Thank you for sprinkling your brilliance all over this book.

To my "Play Maker" contributors, Willie Geist, Nate Berkus, Rob and Kristen Bell, Anthony DeBenedet, Joe Saylor, Liz Gumbinner, Kristen Chase, Bela Gandhi, Laura Harrison Mayes, and Marie LeBaron, thank you so much for adding your amazing voices to my book. You all pretty much rule.

To Heidi Krupp, for encouraging me to run toward publishing my book and giving me sound advice on how to get started.

Thank you to my brilliant book team at HarperCollins: designer Leah Carlson-Stanisic, associate publisher Jen Hart, cover designer Emin Mancheril, marketing guru Molly Waxman, publicist Anwesha Basu, production editor Ivy McFadden, and Andrea Rosen.

To Jonathan, my anchor, most loyal friend, and easily the funniest person I know. Thanks for loving me so hard.

To my dynamic duo, Max and Tru, thanks for clapping as hard for me as I do for you. I love you both beyond measure and am so proud to be your mom.